The Roadway to Heaven

The Roadway to Heaven

—ᴍ—

The True Story of Five Brothers, One Car and A Family Forever Changed

C.C. Hasty Andrews

ISBN: 069288453X
ISBN 13: 9780692884539
Library of Congress Control Number: 2017907553
C.C. Andrews, Shelbyville, TN

August 15, 2015 (Facebook post)
PRAY AND PRAY hard.

My husband, eighteen-year-old son, and I spent the day redecorating my two youngest sons' bedroom. They had decided that they were too old at nine and six years old for bunk beds and wanted their own beds! As I owned a shabby chic furniture store, it was imperative that

I find the two perfect beds for their room. New stuff is junk, just in case y'all were wondering! That week I painted the beds June-bug green and the dresser navy blue with green accents, and I had the perfect accessories picked out. That Sunday I was ready to decorate! It was what I consider the perfect day. I was doing what I loved, in my very own home! My husband P.J. was motivated and excited to help. Our eighteen-year-old son Alex volunteered to help, and we were having a great day getting the room ready for the big reveal. In order for us to surprise the youngest boys, they had gone to stay with their grandparents for the weekend. Around two o'clock, we were close to having the room finished but needed just a little more time. Alex, my son from a previous marriage, didn't want to go to his dad's that day but decided he would so that he could get the boys and bring them home for us while we finished the final details. He had made this very same drive for us many times before.

As a mother, you think that if something happens, you will somehow know or have an indication. I didn't have a clue. At 4:09 p.m., I received a call from the 615 area code. I immediately knew something was wrong. A man explained to me that my son Alex had been in a bad wreck and that I needed to get there as fast as I could. My heart skipped several beats as I asked him if there were other passengers in the vehicle. He told me yes. I knew then that our lives were forever changed. All four boys had been pinned in the vehicle. While obtaining information to locate the scene of the accident, I could hear my son begging to talk to me. As soon as Alex was on the phone he said, "I am so sorry; I tried to stop it," and then he immediately started to list his and his brothers' injuries and begged me to get there as soon as possible. I was amazed at how clear headed this son of mine was, but more about that a little later. I told my husband that we didn't have time to put socks on or change clothes, and I ran to get our twenty-year-old son, our oldest, from his room. We raced to the scene of the accident. Before we arrived at the scene, we knew what had caused the wreck. The rain and warm weather were the perfect cocktail for slick roads. We were having trouble accelerating from stop signs due to lack of traction. Because of the slick road conditions, Alex's vehicle lost traction and started to hydroplane. The oncoming driver of a SUV, seeing Alex's vehicle out of control, veered off the road out of instinct. Unfortunately, it was in the same direction Alex's car was headed. So what do you do in a moment like this? The only thing you can do: pray.

CHAPTER 1

I PRAYED ALL the way to the scene of the accident. I prayed that God would protect my boys. That He would help me stay calm and to know what to do. Somehow, I instantly knew that this would be a long journey, and I would have to be strong through it all. I didn't have to see the car or my kids to know it was bad. When you are told that all four are pinned in the vehicle, you know that it's bad. So all I could do was pray for what was to come.

When we arrived at the scene, my husband and I ran as fast as we could to get to the vehicle. Time slowed down. Time sped up. There is no way to explain it so that the human brain can understand. I had a thousand thoughts in my head, all at one time. My senses became hyper focused. I took in the scene in a simple moment. I couldn't get close to my kids. I knew that to do so would be a distraction to the paramedics. I felt a helplessness that I had never imagined could exist. I knew we needed prayers—and the fastest way to get the word out? Social media. I knew some would think that I was insane for taking the time to take a picture to post on Facebook. The truth is in that moment, time was all I had. I posted a picture of the scene with a caption that read, "Pray and pray hard." The crazy part is that I hated the way that sounded in that moment, but my mind couldn't come up with anything better. Grammar went flying out the window, and my mind could think only in small bursts.

Imagine looking at a vehicle that you should recognize but don't, because it looks like a smashed aluminum can. Try to imagine hearing your kids screaming inside the car, begging for help, but being unable to do a single solitary thing to help them. You can't hold their hands, comfort them, or tell them it will be okay. Because you honestly don't know. Imagine trying to evaluate the damage to the vehicle and trying to prepare yourself for which of them might not make it. I remember thinking that Jacob would probably be the one most critical because he was on the passenger side in the front, where the vehicle took the most impact. I saw Jackson, and since there was no blood anywhere on his body and his eyes were open, I thought he was okay. I had been the most afraid for Jackson on the way to the scene because he was so small. He was the baby of the family. I knew there was the possibility of internal injuries, but my mind refused to process anything except what I could visually see right then in front of me. I started living second to second and in the "now" on the side of that road and from that moment forward.

Josh was extracted first. One down, three to go. "Hurry!" was all I could think over and over in my head. "Get them in the helicopters. What's taking so long?" I noticed a woman with her arms outstretched toward the car my boys were in, praying, who I later learned was the daughter of the passenger from the other vehicle that had been involved in the accident. That was where I needed to be, I thought. By someone who had enough sense to be praying. I didn't know her. It didn't matter. I went close to where she was and knelt in the grass and prayed.

It was there, with my knees pressed into the grass and dirt, that I received an overwhelming peace. "I have this," God whispered to me. "There is a purpose and a plan for this." I knew that the road would be long and my faith would be tested over and over, but I never lost that peace. In the midst of surgeries yet to come, days when I wasn't sure which one of my babies might die, I always knew that God had a plan. As mothers, we seem to think that we are in control. If our children succeed, it is our doing. If they fail, their failures are ours too. If they are smart, well behaved, and respectful, we think we too have accomplished this. When the nurse hands us this swaddled newborn baby at the hospital, it is our duty to take the baby home and keep him or her alive and safe. The truth is, the only one in control is God. My children are His children. He loves them more than even I could ever begin to imagine. His plan for their lives supersedes mine.

One by one, they were extracted from the car. I heard Alex scream only one time, "Please get my brothers out of this car" while his brothers were in the vehicle with him. My heart broke for him because in that moment I realized the emotional battle he would have to face. To this day, I am amazed at the instinct to protect and nurture his brothers this son of mine had. Our three youngest sons are from my husband's previous marriage, but my two oldest sons love them like they have been their brothers since birth. His first and only thought was for his younger brothers. He wasn't initially trapped in the car. He shifted his broken leg and trapped himself further trying

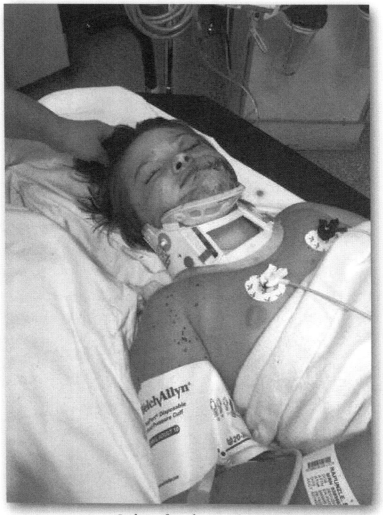

Joshua after the Accident

to reach his brothers in the back seat to remove debris that was on top of them. He comforted his twelve-year-old brother by continuing to talk with him and patting him with his shattered arm. Not until all of his brothers were out of the vehicle did he finally allow himself to scream from the pain he was in. His first instinct when they crashed was to pray to God. He prayed for God to remove their pain, and He did. Alex later told us that after his prayer, everyone in the car became pain free and peace settled around them. I cannot begin to express how proud I am of him. I also later learned that as the car was hydroplaning, God spoke to him and told him, "Do not be afraid." He told Alex that he and his brothers would live.

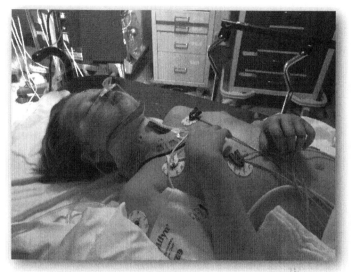

Jacob after the Accident

Alex was the last to be extracted from the car. A paramedic walked up to me and told me to run. Literally. He said that what they were fixing to do would cause Alex to scream worse than I could ever imagine because they would have to set his leg there on the scene without pain medication. If it were him and Alex were his child, he would want someone to warn him. I did the only thing I could do: I ran.

We rushed to the hospital, not knowing what we would discover when we arrived. As we pulled into the parking lot, we saw a helicopter coming in for a landing. At the time, we didn't know which child it was. My mother-in-law called to ask me what I needed her to do. I told her to be there for my husband and to not let him out of her sight. My husband later exclaimed, "So that's why I couldn't ever shake her!" Alex, who had turned eighteen a week before the accident, was taken to the adult hospital, while our three youngest boys were taken to Vanderbilt Children's Hospital. I couldn't be in both places at the same time, and I struggled with this over the next few weeks. My phone became my lifeline between both hospitals.

—∞—

I felt a helplessness that I have never experienced before and pray that I don't ever have to again. I have always been in control in every situation. Now, I had none. My son could lose all of his children, and there was nothing I could do to help him. All I could do was make sure that I was there every step of the way. If he was going to break down, he would not have to do it alone.

Diane Wray, P.J.'s mother

—∞—

August 16, 2015 (Facebook post)
(C.C.)
We are on our way to Vanderbilt in Nashville, TN. They were pinned in the car for a long time. All four boys have been life flighted. All we know is Jackson has a broken arm and Alex Arroyo has a broken arm, leg and hip. They have not told us anything else. I am taking the time to post on Facebook because I believe in the power of prayer and miracles. Please pray for my babies.

Have you ever gotten hurt but were afraid to look at it to see how bad it really was? That was exactly how I felt while being taken back to see Alex at Vanderbilt University Medical Center. I needed to see him for myself, to know that he was okay, but the fear was overwhelming. I kept telling myself, "You can do this. You are strong." The truth was, I didn't have a choice. It was like walking face first into my biggest fear. When I first saw him, my heart exploded with relief and fear, all at the same time. I could see that he had badly broken bones, he was covered in blood, and he had almost bitten his tongue in half, but he was alive. His vitals were all over the place, and nurses and doctors kept rushing in and out. We were then told to wait in the hall while they performed x-rays. The sound of his screaming tore through me. It was a sound that I will never forget. I will admit that I actually ran from the pain of his screams. I just couldn't do it, not yet.

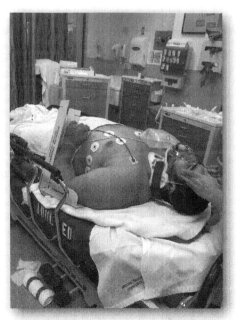

Alex after the Accident

My new best friends were the surgeons as they come to deliver new information. I had always been the mom who was nervous when my children were sick. Why do they have a fever? Can the doctor not give them something to make them feel better? What do you mean we just have to let it run its course? Several years before, Justin hurt his ankle in football practice. The emergency room gave him pain medicine, and I worried the entire time it was in his system. I logically knew that the doctor wouldn't purposely overdose my son and that he would be just fine, but the mom in me was scared to death. This time, I was on board with whatever it would take to mend Alex's body. Surgery? Okay, how fast can we do that? I would count down the hours and minutes until he could have his next dose of pain medicine. Seeing your child suffering and in excruciating pain will definitely change your perspective.

During this time, I was receiving updates on the younger boys by phone as my husband and his family were allowed to see them. Joshua had a severe laceration to his face, a fractured eye socket, broken teeth, internal bleeding, and a broken leg. Jacob had multiple broken bones in all four of his limbs and deep lacerations. I kept asking about Jackson. P.J.'s mother, Diane, and sister Nicole kept telling me, "We haven't been allowed to see him yet." After several hours of waiting, Diane finally called with news. Jackson was being rushed into emergency surgery. They believed he had internal injuries and a possible spinal cord injury. My knees hit the hospital floor right there in the emergency room. Not Jackson! This cannot be happening! It was like a mantra playing over and over in my head. This was one of the only two times I actually fell to my knees.

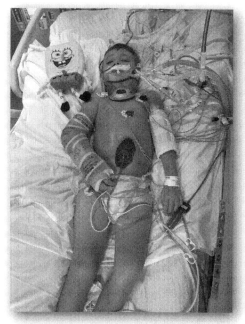

Jackson in the NICU

As soon as Alex was transported to the trauma unit and in stable condition, I ran to Vanderbilt Children's Hospital. Literally. The two hospitals were several blocks from each other. This route would be made over and over throughout the next few weeks. I was taken back to see Jacob and Joshua. They were both black and blue from head to toe. Joshua's entire face was swollen and bleeding. Jacob had severe lacerations and broken bones everywhere. They were both heavily medicated but able to talk to us. This was the first time I was able to witness just how strong and brave our boys were. Jacob tried to make jokes with me. Joshua refused pain medication. To this day, I am overwhelmed with pride at how strong our boys were.

—ɯ—

We were so amazed at how much the Rutherford County paramedics, fire fighters, and emergency staff cared for our boys. Not only did they visit them in the hospital after the accident, but they stayed up to date on our boys' progress as they healed. We were later told that they were amazed at how respectful and polite our boys were on the scene.

P.J., the boys' dad

—ɯ—

All of the family met in a conference room. It was there that P.J., my husband, announced that he wanted to make it clear that he would not tolerate anyone blaming Alex for the accident, and anyone who did so could leave the hospital. He explained to them that it was just an accident and could have happened to anyone, including him if he had been driving. His ex-wife's family had made a statement that was overheard by a member of my husband's family that let my husband know it needed to be addressed quickly. I hadn't even considered that people would think that the accident was Alex's fault until that moment. People even commented on Facebook and private messaged me in the weeks following the accident asking me who was at fault for the accident, hinting toward the other driver being under the influence. There were all kinds of insane accusations, which is to be expected in a small town. We heard later there was a rumor going around Alex's high school that he was on drugs while driving. To make it clear now, Alex was completely sober per the mandatory blood test he was given at the hospital. The family in the other vehicle were wonderful Christian people who followed the progress of our boys with continued prayer. It was an accident. One that could not be avoided and just simply happened.

—⚬—

The owners of the home the accident occurred in front of later said that there have been over fifty wrecks in front of their home since they have lived there. A young high school girl had also lost her life there.

C.C., the boys' mother

—⚬—

As Alex and the boys were coming home and only ten minutes from our house, the back tire of his vehicle hit a gravel patch due to road erosion on the inside of a curve, which caused his vehicle to hydroplane. The oncoming SUV, seeing his vehicle hydroplane, took the ditch out of instinct. They actually met head on in front of someone's yard, not on the road. Alex was driving under the speed limit and did absolutely nothing wrong. They were all wearing seat belts. He was not on his phone or distracted, as his brothers assured us later. As I stated before, the warm weather and earlier rain created the perfect cocktail for slippery roads. My husband and I slid all over the road on the way to the scene of the accident. In order to get traction accelerating from a stop sign, my husband would have to press the gas, let up, and press it again. In no way could Alex have avoided this accident. We were later told by the homeowners where the accident occurred that there had been over fifty accidents in that curve, and a high school student had lost her life.

Even knowing this, I knew my son would hurt for a long time. Alex has always been my child who loved everyone, defending those weaker than him. His heart is tremendously huge, and with that comes a sense of responsibility and burden. I would soon learn that no matter what we said or did, this was something that God intended him to walk through on his own. As a mother, I wanted to shelter, protect, and defend him. I wanted to fix the boo-boos and make everything in his life okay. It was hard for me to accept that I couldn't heal his heart. I now know only God could do that. This was Alex's part of the journey, and God was and is molding him into the man he will someday become.

CHAPTER 2

*Do not be afraid, for I have ransomed you. I have
called you by name, you are mine. When you go
through deep waters, I will be with you. When you
go through rivers of difficulty, you will not drown.
When you walk through the fire of oppression, you
will not be burned: the flames will not consume you.*

ISAIAH *43:1–2 NLT*

MINUTES FELT LIKE hours, and hours felt like days. Yet everything moved in fast forward. Later that night, I was able to sleep a couple of hours in the chair in the waiting room of the trauma unit. I felt ashamed that it was a relief that I could not constantly be in the trauma unit with Alex but could only visit him for ten minutes every hour. My heart needed those fifty minutes to recover from the ten minutes spent with him. He was in such excruciating agony from having his leg put in traction, and there was nothing I could do to take it away. Traction is the use of weights to forcefully pull on the leg to keep it in a straight position before surgery can be performed. He later told me he didn't remember much from his time in the trauma unit except the memory of pain. I remember every excruciating minute, hour, and day.

I can remember watching movies, hearing stories, and reading books where parents were faced with their children in similar life-and-death situations, and I couldn't imagine myself going through those situations. Yet here I was, in the middle of my worst fears. With not only one child, but four. I had to tell myself repeatedly to be strong. I had to remind myself that if I broke down, I couldn't be there for them, and that simply was not an option. I was mom. It was my job to protect, nurture, and provide for them. I knew I would have to make decisions, and I had to make the right ones.

—∞—

The drive to the hospital was one of the longest drives in my entire life. I immediately started making phone calls to make arrangements for our animals and to notify family members about what had happened. This would be my role throughout the next several months. I was the one who got things done. It was impossible for me stand still for too long, much less sit. In many ways, having to walk back and forth the several blocks between the adult hospital and Vanderbilt Children's Hospital was a blessing. It allowed me to walk off excess energy. I just felt I needed to be moving at all times. It was definitely a supernatural strength, because when I look back on it now, it exhausts me simply thinking about it.

C.C., the boys' mom

—∞—

Every other hour, I would alternate the ten minutes we could spend with Alex with his father, Carlos. This way we could sleep for at least two hours at a time. The first week I slept maybe two or three hours a night in bursts. I was simply too afraid that one of the boys would need me. Each time I woke up, the reality of everything that was happening would come racing back in fast forward.

That night, Jackson needed exploratory surgery to determine the extent of the internal injuries, but the medical team had to quickly close him up shortly after the surgery began. They were unable to perform the surgery because his vitals dropped, and they were afraid of losing him. We discovered that his colon had ruptured and he had broken all the lower vertebra in his back from the force of the impact and his seat belt. Had he not had the seat belt on, he most assuredly would have died during the accident. The same seat belt that saved his life also caused all of Jackson's injuries. As long as Jackson was alive, his body could heal. That was all that mattered in that moment. Jackson was alive.

August 17, 2015 (Facebook post)

While I have a moment, I want to give everyone a quick update. First, we are humbled by the love and support from family, friends and even strangers. The outpouring of love and support has been staggering. Your prayers are being heard and felt, so please keep them coming. First, because it is hard to continue to answer this question, Alex picked up the boys from their grandparents and due to slick road conditions, was in a head-on-collision. We are not sure as to the exact details of the accident yet and to be honest, it doesn't matter. Joshua and Jacob both have broken bones, lacerations, and minor injuries. They are tough as nails. They have already shown Gods miraculous healing by making the progress they have. Alex made it through surgery today and we are waiting to learn the extent of his injuries. He is okay, and has shown such strength and love for his brothers. While trapped and broken in the car, he never cried. He comforted his bothers and loved on them, even with his arm brutally broken. Jackson is in critical condition. We are taking it day by day. We have had bad test results, but he also has doctors that believe in God, and the miracle of healing. He is scheduled for surgery tomorrow. We have already watched God work. Broken bones that required surgery suddenly only need boots. Casts are being removed because they no longer need them. So please, believe with us that we will continue to see Him work miracles for our boys. Please be patient with us and know that we will share updates when we can as we know so many of you love them as much as we do.

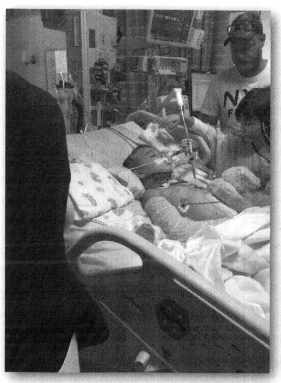

Joshua Saying Goodbye to Jackson
Before Leaving the Hospital

—⚉—

When I got to the hospital, I was taken back to see Jacob and Joshua. No one could tell me where Jackson was, so I knew something was seriously wrong. Finally, after what felt like several hours, I caught a glimpse of him. He was on a metal table being rolled down the hall with numerous nurses and doctors around him. They rolled him into a room and immediately closed the white curtain. A nurse stood guard outside of the room and refused to let me see him. So, I sat across from the room staring at that white curtain, praying that Jackson would live.

The surgeon finally came to me and asked where Jackson's mom was. I told him that she was at the adult Vanderbilt Hospital with our other son because I thought he was speaking about my wife. At this point, the boy's mother was on her way from Ohio. She hadn't seen them in several months, but I knew that they needed her now more than ever. He explained that Jackson was a very sick little boy and had internal injuries, so they would have to perform exploratory surgery immediately. I told him to do whatever he needed to do to save my son's life.

I asked the surgeon to let me see him before they took him back, and he told me that I had only a minute with him because every second meant life and death. He looked lifeless lying there on that metal bed. I can't explain how helpless I felt in that moment. At first glance, he looked as if nothing should be wrong with him at all. He had only one little scratch on his forehead. I asked Jackson, "You okay, buddy?" He opened his eyes and shook his head yes. I told him that I loved him, and he mumbled, "I love you" back to me. That's Jackson for you! Here he was comforting me! It was my first indication that Jackson would have a lot to teach me about strength, courage, and determination. I wouldn't see him open his eyes again for a very long time.

It was after midnight before they let us know that he was in the NICU. He was covered in wires and tubes that were hooked to various machines to help keep him alive. A ventilator had to help him breathe. His whole body was shaking from being cold, or perhaps the trauma. I'm not sure. I could finally see where they had opened his stomach up and could clearly see where the seat belt had injured him. His arm was in a cast. I stayed by Jackson's side, only leaving long enough to check on my other two boys.

P.J., the boys' father

—⁂—

The next morning, Alex was rushed into surgery to repair his crushed arm and broken femur. I was torn between gratefulness that his pain would be alleviated and fear of him having to go through surgery. In the main lobby, there was a TV that listed each patient's name in alphabetical order and the status of his or her surgery. I couldn't help but watch for Alex's name. I was also given a pager, just like the one you receive at restaurants while waiting for a table to open up. Each time it buzzed in my hand, my heart skipped a few beats and my feet hit the ground running. I hoped for good news and tried to prepare myself for bad.

Alex's surgery was a success, or so we thought. As soon as I visited him in the recovery room, I knew something was wrong. His arm was in even more pain than before he went into surgery. I hoped that this was typical and that it would hurt worse before it got better. Luckily, his friends had come to visit, and I happily let them go back to sit with him. It was so hard seeing him in so much pain. He was able to push through the pain so much more with his friends around.

As the day wore on, we quickly realized that something wasn't right. He screamed, he begged, he pleaded—with us, the nurses, the doctors, with anyone who would listen. Finally, the next morning, the morning-shift nurse took over. He actually listened to me.

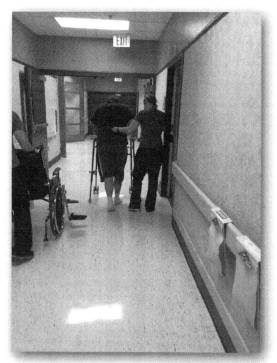

Alex Walking for the First Time

Really listened. I came to depend on him and the knowledge he provided over the next few days. He understood our concerns and made us believe that he truly did care about Alex's welfare. I will be forever grateful for those nurses who didn't just dismiss our concerns. He immediately called Alex's orthopedic surgeon. We discovered that Alex was suffering from a very serious condition called acute compartment syndrome. This occurs after a traumatic injury and causes a severe high pressure in the compartment or area of injury, which results in insufficient blood supply to muscles and nerves. If untreated, the lack of blood supply leads to permanent muscle and nerve damage and can cause the patient to lose the limb. Alex once again had to be rushed back into surgery.

August 18, 2015 (Facebook post)

Quick update: Alex had to have emergency surgery this morning and is now in recovery. Please pray for God to help control his pain level and negate the negative effects of medication. Jackson was not able to have surgery today. The doctors are trying to get him stable first. Pray that his vitals stay good and we can move on to the next step. Thanks for all of your love and support.

Thankfully, the orthopedic surgeon did not have to cut Alex's carpal tunnel nerve, and he believed that they had caught the acute compartment syndrome in time. Because of the severe swelling, they had to leave his arm open and use a wound vac. This is basically a vacuum that is attached to the wound to help promote healing. As you can imagine, this too was added pain that Alex would have to endure for the next week.

CHAPTER 3

*Be Strong and courageous. Do not be afraid or
terrified because of them, for the Lord your God goes
with you; he will never leave you or forsake you.*

DEUTERONOMY *31:6 NIV*

THE VERY NEXT morning was one of the most difficult for me. By
this point, the pull from the adult hospital to Vanderbilt Children's
Hospital was wearing on me. I would love to say that I was super-
mom and spent equal amounts of time with each of them. I simply
couldn't. My family was very small, so I had to spend more time
with Alex, whereas my husband had a very large family that could
be there with him and our youngest three boys. My husband spent
most of his time with Jackson, who was the most critically injured.
Thankfully, the other family members were able to fill in where
my husband and I couldn't. If it weren't for them, I'm not sure
what we would have done. We both made sure to spend time with
each of our children every day. They all needed to know that they
were loved, that they would be okay, and that we thought they were
tough and brave. We encouraged them to take their medicine and
do what the doctors and nurses asked them to do. It was important
that they know where we were and that we were just a phone call

away. And trust me, they definitely let us know when they needed us. There were days I would walk/run between hospitals at least fifteen or more times. I would be at Alex's bedside and get a call from my husband that one of the doctors wanted to speak with us. I would get a call from Jacob saying that he wanted to see me, or a call from Joshua just to chitchat. Every time they called, I literally ran.

—◊◊—

My sister-n-law Casey gave me a backpack with toiletries early on. It would be a vital part of me. Because I had to travel so much between hospitals and only had waiting rooms to sleep in, I carried that backpack everywhere. To this day, I still carry one instead of a purse.

C.C., the boys' mother

—◊◊—

August 19, 2015 (Facebook post)
Jackson is scheduled to have surgery this morning. Pray that his vitals stay good and that God guides the surgeons' hands to repair everything that needs to be repaired. In fact, pray that it goes even better than they expect! I cannot express how much the support and love everyone has shown us means. Even though we may not be able to respond to every message, comment and post, know that in those rare moments when we have a chance to look, we are encouraged by reading them. No one ever expects to be here in this moment, but we are and the prayers and love are helping to get us through.

It was day three, and Jackson was finally able to have surgery. The doctors prepared us: he might not live through the surgery. His injures were severe, and although his vitals were still not good enough for surgery, his body had started to show signs of infection. Surgery was no longer an option, but a necessity. As afraid as I was for all my boys, that fear never held par with the fear I felt as Jackson went into surgery. I always knew where I stood with our other boys. "This is the injury; this is how we fix it." With Jackson, it was completely unknown. We knew that his colon had ruptured, causing internal injuries. We also knew at this point that he had broken all his lower vertebrae, and they would have to be fused during surgery. There were also a lot of unknowns. Would his vitals stay strong enough to continue with surgery? What else would they discover once they opened him up? Would he live?

I couldn't face sitting in the waiting room watching a screen with names rolling over and over with updates again. I couldn't sit in a waiting room with family members I hardly knew and some I didn't even like very much. So I sat in the parking garage for hours waiting for the phone call. I prayed. I cried. I pleaded with God to let him live. To let him stay with us. It really was all I could do. When it was close to time for Jackson's surgery to be over, I went to be with Jacob and Joshua.

As I was visiting Joshua, my phone rang. It was my husband. I went into the hallway so that I could hear him. When the buzzing in my ears finally calmed down enough for me to hear him, I hit my knees. This was the last time I would do so. He had lived, and the surgery had been successful. The doctors had been able to clean out the infection and fuse his lower spine! Luckily, my sister-n-law received a text message letting her know that Jackson was okay at the same time I received the call, or I probably would have scared everyone in the room senseless. They initially thought the news was bad due to my reaction, but the text message allowed everyone to know that everything was okay. Jackson's grandfather bent down and hugged me, telling me over and over that Jack was okay. My reaction was not fear, but pure, simple relief. I was overcome with happiness, and I couldn't stop crying or shaking. Finally, Jackson's grandfather was able to help me walk to the waiting room, where my husband was waiting for me. It was the first time in days that we smiled when we saw each other. Jackson was alive! There were more surgeries to come and many more days ahead that we would be afraid for his life, but at that moment, he was alive. It was enough.

August 19, 2015 (Facebook post)

I'm sorry I am just now posting, but I have been with Alex Arroyo and haven't had the chance until now. Biggest praise report of all, Jackson is out of surgery and the surgeon said everything went great! Better even than expected, but we all know that was God's plan! He still has surgeries ahead, so continue to pray for miracles. Until now I haven't asked for prayers for myself, but I and Carlos need them as well. It is hard to watch your child in so much pain, and not be able to help him. So please lift us and all of our family in your prayers. I can't stress enough how much your prayers are making a difference. Miracles are happening!

Before I saw Jackson's mom after his surgery, my husband told me that I needed to be prepared. She had left during his surgery to get "dressed up." Literally. Hair, makeup, clothes, the whole routine. I was absolutely floored. While I had been in a parking garage plead- ing with God for Jackson's life, she had left to put makeup on. I simply couldn't imagine a mother who would even think to do this. I wouldn't have left that hospital if someone offered me a billion dollars and my own private island. There was nothing that would cause me to leave my babies. Not to mention to take the time to put makeup on. At that point, I had taken one shower, and someone had finally brought me fresh clothing the day before. It took literally everything I had in me to walk away from her and control my anger. This wasn't the time or place to have a confrontation with her, and even if I did, it wouldn't have accomplished anything. You can't talk with a drug addict. There is no reasoning with them. I decided that if she didn't put them in harm's way, I would keep my thoughts to myself. Unfortunately, she did exactly that the very next day.

The next morning I went to visit Jackson, and she was bent over his bed. This didn't concern me. What did concern me was that she was stumbling over the cords that were attached to him keeping him alive, literally trying to move them so that she could "kiss" him. I made her stop immediately. I looked at my mother-in-law, who was sitting behind his bed, and she mouthed, "Yes, she is," confirming that she was under the influence of drugs. I mouthed, "She is getting out right now!"

My husband came into the room and knew immediately that she was on drugs. He asked me to take care of it. My solution: call the police. I wasn't going to get into a physical altercation right there in the hospital, which was what the outcome would have been had I confronted her. So, I called Vanderbilt Security.

While waiting for them, my mother-in-law convinced the boy's mother to leave the room and let Jackson rest. When the officer arrived, I explained to him that their mother was addicted to drugs and didn't need to be around the boys while under the influence. I wanted it documented and on file. I wanted to know that should we have to call them again, they would be aware of the circumstances. At first, he really wasn't taking me seriously, but I said something that caused him to realize who I was. He looked at me and exclaimed, "My God, it's you!" By this time we had been featured on several of our local news channels. Our family literally broke records, according to the nurses, for having the most children LifeFlighted in critical condition at one time to Vanderbilt. Definitely not a record we wanted to break! He immediately assured me that he would let everyone in the security department know our situation and assured me that the next time I called them, they would arrest her for child endangerment. I did not want to have to do this under any circumstance. She is their mother. The boys needed her and the comfort she could provide them. But to keep my kids safe, I would absolutely call security in a heartbeat. It came to a point that she was not allowed in the boy's room without another family member being present with her. They all knew she was addicted to drugs and although it was important to have her there with them, it was more important that the boys were safe. A couple of months after Jackson was released from the hospital, she put Jackson at risk while under the influence. We were forced to once again cut off all contact between her and the boys. Thankfully, that was the wake-up call she needed. She finally admitted she had a drug problem and got sober. I pray that she continues to stay drug free for her sons because they love her and need her in their lives.

CHAPTER 4

*Rejoice in hope, be patient in tribulation,
be constant in prayer.*

ROMANS 12:12 ESV

August 20, 2015 (Facebook post)

THIS BABY (JACKSON) *didn't want us to leave his room. Every time we stopped talking to him he opened his eyes to find us! Pray today that his fever goes down and that they can make him more comfortable. Joshua also has a fever and will need a small procedure today so pray that the infection is removed and he is healed. Alex is scheduled for surgery tomorrow so pray for the surgeons and a successful outcome. He also has a fever and we are believing for no infection. Again, thank you so much for your love, prayers and support!*

It seemed that every time we felt we had a handle on their diagnosis and that they were making progress, a setback would happen. It was like a volleyball game—a diagnosis would be given, then taken back. They would be in stable condition, and then something would happen, and we would once again worry about something new the doctors had found. This was the opportunity for God to show up and show out! We would be told that a broken bone would require surgery, only to find out hours later that it didn't need surgery after all. We would be told that exploratory surgery was needed, only to be told an hour later that the labs were wrong. Fevers would come and then miraculously leave. I am still grateful to this day to have had a front row seat to watch the power of prayer and faith work in action.

August 20, 2015 (Facebook post)
(P.J.)
Update. Jacob Andrews is going to be released today around 3:30pm. He is going to be in the care of his grandparents. So, keep them in your prayers and any support they may need. And once again I appreciate all the support!

When I received the call that Jacob was to be released from the hospital, my first reaction was fear. I needed him with us. I needed him near and under the care of the nurses. What if something went wrong? Would his grandparents know how to handle it? I had absolute faith in them, but after experiencing such a traumatic, life-altering event, I wanted to cling that much closer. God had to remind me that He was in control. He was always in control, and I needed to extend my faith that much farther.

Jacob Leaving the Hospital

—⁂—

Our boys did everything together. You never saw one without the other. If one of them got in trouble, the other one was quick to come to his defense. If one was sick, the other two would go into caretaker mode, fetching tissues, drinks, food, or whatever they thought would help their brother. Their bond is stronger than anything I have ever seen. After the accident, the first thing every single one of them asked was, "How are my brothers?" It was hard seeing the fear they had for their brothers, especially for Alex and Jackson. The first couple of days after the accident, Jacob and Joshua were on separate floors. After having to repeatedly wheel each brother to the other's room several times a day, the nurses decided to make a way for them to be on the same floor. Jackson was in the NICU; otherwise, I'm sure they would have been on the same floor as him as well!

P.J., the boys' dad

—⚋—

August 21, 2015 (Facebook post)

We will again have Jackson and Alex in surgery today. Pray that God guides the surgeons' hands to create miracles and for NO MORE complications. It is time for our baby's breakthrough and for God to shine in the operating room. Pray that God comforts our boys and keeps them from being anxious. Also pray for us parents as we need peace as well through this day. We have faith and believe He is in control, but we are also human with human fears too. I cannot begin to express how much comfort it brings knowing there is an army of prayer warriors out there believing with us for our boys! Thank you for your prayers, love and support!

The doctors discovered an abscess caused by the seatbelt on Jackson's tummy. It had scabbed over, so the doctors were unaware of it initially. His fever and white blood cell count alerted the doctors to search for what could be causing his symptoms. It would have to be cleaned out and a wound vac applied. Alex had to have a skin graft done in order to cover the wound on his arm from the acute compartment syndrome.

By this point, we started to notice a trend. If Jackson had a fever, so did Alex. If Alex had to have surgery, so did Jackson. Every time I was allowed back to see Alex, he would ask what was wrong with Jackson. I would tell him that everything was okay, and he would accuse me of lying. He asked anyone who came to visit him the same question. "What is wrong with Jackson?" I asked him later how he knew that something was wrong with Jackson, and he said he could feel it in his heart. We chose not to tell him until he was released from the trauma unit, under the advice of his doctor. We knew he simply couldn't handle the stress of it. It was the one and only time I have ever lied to my son.

August 21, 2015 (Facebook post)
The devil has been swinging full force today. My assistant called today to tell me that the owner of the building at my store had a real estate company at Vintage Charm putting a for sale sign up, then I am told someone expects me to take care of a flat tire from Vanderbilt that they received from pulling into the store parking lot. I am later told that our GoFundMe account has been reported as offensive on Facebook. But guess what???? The devil is a liar and God's got this! Our babies are out of surgery, alive and breathing! The surgeons said vitals are even better than when they started! Our God is awesome and He is listening to all of our prayers!

August 21, 2015 (Facebook post)
Anyone near Vanderbilt that could bring us a small mini fan tonight?!?! Verizon didn't pull through so no phone but at least we could get him this. Please?!!?!

The skin graft on Alex's leg caused him extreme amounts of pain. The doctor told him it would feel like a severe sunburn, and Alex said the pain was nothing like a sunburn, so he didn't believe doctors much after that.

I was amazed at how quickly people responded to any requests that we made. It so happened that my good friend LouAnn Smith was only a few blocks away from Vanderbilt, and she delivered the fan to me that very evening. It was such a huge blessing over the next few weeks as the cool air from the fan made the pain from the skin graft site bearable for him.

August 22, 2015 (Facebook post)

Take a moment today to pray for this kid too (Justin)! He has been my rock since day one. He has hardly left the hospital, slept in chairs and on the floor with me, and done it while not feeling good himself. So, take a moment to love on him and pray for his healing and strength. Thanks and we love everyone!

Our oldest son, Justin, was such a huge blessing to me. As I have mentioned before, my family is very small. The first week after the accident, Justin never left the hospital. I cannot imagine going through something like that completely alone, and I was so very proud of him for stepping up and being the son and brother that he was.

Alex saw P.J. several days later, for the first time after the accident. Alex immediately had a severe panic attack and had to be heavily sedated. It was difficult for Alex because he believed that P.J. would blame him for the accident. In turn, it was difficult for my husband to be around Alex because he saw the pain it caused Alex. P.J. later shared that deep down there was a small part of him that did blame Alex, so he only came to visit Alex twice in the hospital. I

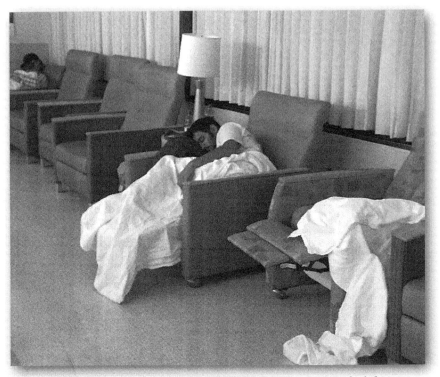

Justin Sleeping in the Trauma Waiting Room at Vanderbilt

understood his feelings, and had the tables been reversed, I cannot say that I wouldn't have felt the same. His emotions were all over the place, just as mine were. There were times that I resented my husband for asking Alex to go get the boys that fateful day. Neither feelings were logical, but we cannot always control how we feel.

It was also during this time that irreparable damage was done to my extended family. My uncle and his children simply chose not to call or visit until a week after the accident. I couldn't comprehend how they would choose not to be there for Alex or me. My uncle passed away before we could reconcile, and to be honest, I don't think we ever would have. Family should show up when it matters most, and some of my family simply did not. I was thankful for my mom and brother, who did.

I was also extremely disappointed in the lack of support from friends whom I would have expected to be there. You learn very quickly when something like this happens who your true friends are. Friends should be the first ones to show up. They should make time to be there for you, especially when something as cata-strophic as this accident happens. Nothing hurts more than real-izing that the single person you thought would always be by your side is not going to be there as you had been when that person needed you.

However, I was amazed at the support from people we didn't know personally. The care packages, donations, texts, e-mails, and phone calls were simply amazing, and our family was so thankful to have them. It was a reminder that although I felt alone at times, I really had support from our community.

It was important to me that Alex always have someone with him, even if that person was just in the waiting-room area. Alex needed to be in contact with his father and me at all times. Thankfully, I had an iPad Mini that he could use. We believed his iPhone had been de-stroyed in the accident. He couldn't call us, but he could FaceTime me or his father whenever he needed us. As we couldn't go into the trauma unit after hours, it was a great way for him to know we were close by and for him to tell us when he needed things so we could let the nurses know. I'm sure they thought about throwing the iPad in the trash a time or two! I was the only one he would allow to help him to the bathroom or change his clothes, so I needed to be close by at all times. I loved having him accessible, but there were times, too, that I dreaded those calls. He would need me and I simply couldn't get to him, or he would be in pain and there would be nothing I could do to help him.

August 22, 2015 (Facebook post)

God is so good! Jackson is off the breathing machine and sitting up! Only a day after surgery and way before they thought he would. Why? Because we have prayer warriors on our side!

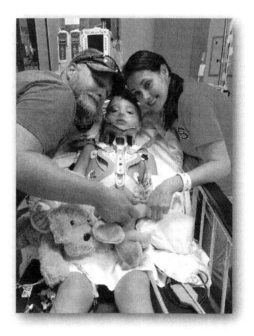

There were so many times that doctors were amazed by the progress our boys made. I had front-row seats to watch God in action! We prayed, expecting God to work. Most times, when we look back on our prayers, we will see that He did indeed answer them—usually in His own time and in His own way. I witnessed time after time prayers that were immediately answered and with no scientific explanation other than God had answered them.

August 22, 2015 (Facebook post)
As soon as Jackson could talk the first person this baby asked about was his big brother Alex, and he had a message for him…

As I have said before, the connection between Jackson and Alex was incredible to watch. Jackson wanted to tell Alex he loved him, so we took a video to show Alex. I cannot express the happiness I saw on Alex's face when he watched the video for the first time. Until this point, I believe that Alex was truly afraid that Jackson had not survived the accident. It gave Alex strength to push through, and he would say on multiple occasions that if Jackson could do it, so could he.

August 23, 2015 (Facebook post)
We had a rough night with Alex but he is finally resting. Please continue to pray for him as he will have the wound vac on until Tuesday or Wednesday. He told me last night how much God helped him through and gave him peace during the wreck. I am so thankful that he believes and loves God. His faith inspires me even more in mine. Joshua may get to go home today. Pray for the infection to leave his body and for a breakthrough. The boys want to be with each other and I know God will make it happen. Continue to pray for Jackson and miraculous healing. I can't wait for our baby to show these doctors that MRI's are wrong and God is right! I am humbled by the support and love

that has been shown to us by our community and even perfect strangers. It is because of you that P.J. and I are making it through this! People keep asking us how we are standing on our feet, the answer is simple…God and the love from everyone who has us covered in prayers. So, keep them coming!

—⚎—

From the very beginning, we were comforted by people reaching out, telling us that the boys were being covered in prayers. There was an army of prayer warriors on their knees praying for our children from every single state in the United States, as well as in several other countries. I was surprised at how quickly our story spread and how it touched people's lives. Knowing that our story was in the hearts of people everywhere gave us hope. I knew that God heard every single prayer and heaven was being flooded with them! I began to see that we were a part of God's greater plan, and this was bigger than even our family could begin to imagine.

P.J., the boys' dad

—⚎—

August 23, 2015 (Facebook post)

Today marks one week since our lives were forever changed. I will no longer say that this is a nightmare, it isn't. Our babies are alive and breathing. We could be planning four funerals. God has blessed us with amazingly strong and brave children, and He has giving us more time to be their parents. How AWESOME is that??? In fact, God is so good…another baby is going home TONIGHT!!!! Just two more to get home so we can all be together again!

August 23, 2015 (Facebook post)
(P.J.)

Update. Josh went home today. He even rolled his own wheelchair out. How about that!?!

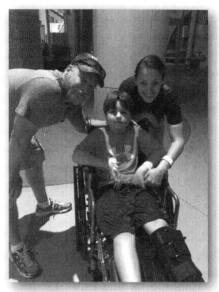

Joshua Leaving the Hospital

August 24, 2015 (Facebook post)

Specific prayer request this morning: pray that Jacksons fever breaks this morning. Pray that Alex is able to eat and hold down food. Please also pray for our two boys that are home and the family members who are taking care of them while we can't. Prayers work, our boys are living breathing proof!

August 24, 2015 (Facebook post)

For everyone who prayed, God answered! Jackson's fever is down and Alex has been able to eat today! Today has been a great day Just maybe P.J. and I will be able to sleep a little tonight.

August 25, 2015 (Facebook post)

Today both Jackson and Alex will have surgical procedures. Please pray that our boys are brave and without pain. One of the hardest things I have ever experienced in my lifetime is to see our babies hurt on this level, and not be able to fix it or make it go away. Please continue to pray for them and us as we take each day minute by minute and hour by hour.

August 25, 2015 (Facebook post)

Both surgical procedures went well and they are finally resting. I seriously have the bravest kids on the planet!

August 29, 2015 (Facebook post)
(P.J.)

I am doing this kind of early. Happy birthday to my sweet little boy Jackson. I feel so bad that he will not enjoy his birthday tomorrow like he normally would. But I can promise you one thing little Jack, we will throw you a huge party when you get better along with your brothers and family. I love you little dude and I will never leave your side.

August 26, 2015 (Facebook post)

Today Jackson turns seven years old. Although celebrating this day in a hospital isn't ideal, a week ago we were not sure this day would get to come, so celebrate we will! I have always been a half glass empty person. Didn't rely on anyone, even God, for anything. I was a fighter, tough, and could take care of my own. My biggest lesson so far through this…I am no one. I don't have this. But God, He is EVERYTHING, and He definitely has this! I have learned that I can't do everything alone. I need friends, family, and our community. Most of all, I need our prayers warriors, as I tend to think of everyone who stays connected with our story to pray. Today's prayer request is to pray that

Jackson's infection leaves his body so that we can prepare to go to Shepherds in Atlanta. Pray that Alex gets to go to Vanderbilt Stallworth Rehabilitation Hospital so that we can start the next phase of his recovery. Also pray for P.J. and I, as we continue to spend time in two separate buildings separated from each other. Thank you and we love each and every one you!

August 26, 2015 (Facebook post)

Praise report: Alex is going to Stallworth today! God is moving mountains and paving the way for miracles. Continue to pray for healing, and NO MORE surgeries, as we found out yesterday that it was a possibility. But God is bigger and His reports are always right!

—⟨⟩—

CHAPTER 5

Jesus told him, "Stand up, pick up your mat, and walk!"

JOHN 5:8 NLT

August 26, 2015 (Facebook post)
ANYONE NEAR VANDERBILT *willing to take me to Verizon? It's about 3.5 miles from here. Or get me a Verizon Sims card and I pay you for it?*

I had promised Alex I would replace his phone, as that was all that he had asked for. Verizon completely lied about replacing his phone, so I had to order a replacement from our insurance company, which took several days. I finally had the phone in my hand, and it wouldn't work! I asked my husband to take me to Verizon, which was a very short distance from the hospital. He literally screamed at me for being selfish and wanting to get Alex a phone. Up until this point, I had put every feeling of abandonment to the side. I had repeatedly asked my husband to come visit Alex so that Alex would see that P.J. wasn't blaming him for the accident, with no success. I felt alone and betrayed. This was the beginning of the divide between my husband and me, and it would only get wider as the next few months passed.

August 27, 2015 (Facebook post)
Please take a moment today to pray that all infection leaves Jacksons body.
Pray also that the cat scans performed this morning go better than expected.
We need our boy to feel better so that we can get him up and WALKING soon!
Pray that Alex has a wonderful first full day at Stallworth. I know we ask for a
lot of prayers but we need y'all to keep them coming!

August 27, 2015 (Facebook post)
Jacksons surgery went well today. They cleaned out a lot of the infection and
applied two wound vacs. He is now back in the NICU where he will receive
24-hour care. The doctors are adamant that he will be okay, but have told us
to expect a longer recovery. A lot of people have asked about the diagnosis of
paralysis. Our answer to this is yes, that is a possibility. He does have a spinal
injury. However, we do not speak it, nor do we believe it. He has shown us
signs that God is in the miracle business and we believe Jackson will have one
heck of a testimony to share one day. We cannot begin to express how grateful
we are for all of the money donated on our behalf on the GoFundMe account
and given to us and just how much it is needed as we continue to stay with
our babies.

By this point, we knew that Jackson had suffered a back injury as
well as a possible spinal cord injury. He had broken all of the lower
vertebrae in his lower spine, which would later have to be fused
back together with metal plates. He was awake enough to complete the initial test upon his arrival to the hospital in which the
doctor places a sharp object against different areas of his body to
determine if there is any feeling. He failed the test several times.
The CT scan was imperative to determine whether Jackson had

a spinal cord injury and if so how extensive the damage was. My husband, mother-in-law, and I were sitting in Jackson's room anxiously awaiting the test results as a team of doctors came into the room.

As the doctor was speaking about Jackson's test results, she casually commented, "We already knew he was paralyzed, so the test didn't provide any new information."

As she continued to speak, I sat there trying to process the words she had just said. I suddenly blurted out, "Wait—he's paralyzed? As in he won't ever walk again? No, we definitely did not know this. That is why we were told we were doing the CT scan today."

You could hear a pin drop in the room. It was completely silent. She apologized, stating that she thought the neurologist had already spoken to us about the results. I'm not sure there is really a good way to learn that your child is paralyzed, but that definitely wasn't the way I would have liked to be told: a doctor casually inserting it into a conversation.

It was the second time I cried, and the only time I did so in front of others. My heart literally broke into a million pieces. His life flashed before my eyes. Him being in a wheelchair. Not being able to walk, jump, run, or play. He would never play sports like his older brothers. Possibly never marry or have children. I would never see him walk again. I also thought about the impact this would have on Alex. I knew that he would blame himself for this, and my heart broke for both of my boys.

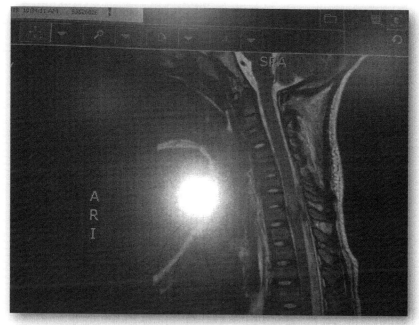

MRI Image Showing Jackson's T1 Spinal Cord Injury

I simply couldn't wrap my head around it. In auto accidents, medical professionals are always concerned with spinal cord injuries. I simply thought that it was a concern but not really likely. I just couldn't believe it would ever happen to one of our boys. Yet here I was, being told that Jackson had a spinal cord injury and would never walk again. It was like living in a nightmare.

We asked to have a meeting with his neurologist as soon as possible. He showed us the images from the CT scan and pointed out where the spinal cord was damaged. He explained that Jackson had a complete T1 spinal cord injury—complete because he had no feeling below the spinal cord tear. Although he believed that kids often defied the odds, he said there was little probability that Jackson would ever walk again. He believed that Jackson had most likely sustained the spinal cord injury from wearing his seat belt. He explained that Jackson's head was still larger than his neck and that he was literally at the perfect age for this to happen. The force of the impact during the accident jerked his neck suddenly forward, causing his spinal cord to tear. However, had he not been wearing his seat belt, he most definitely would not have survived. The one thing that saved his life also caused the most damage to his body.

—◊◊—

The last time I remember walking, I was walking with Jesus.

Jackson

—◊◊—

Those first few weeks after his diagnosis were also the most confusing. Every time his foot kicked or his leg moved, we saw it as a good sign. We poured ourselves into learning everything we could about spinal cord injuries. We would later learn at Scottish Rite Children's Healthcare of Atlanta that those movements meant Jackson was coming out of spinal shock. When someone first receives a spinal cord injury, all of the reflexes below the level of the injury stop, sometimes for several weeks.

We decided to not discuss Jackson's spinal cord injury publicly until Alex was told. I had promised myself that I would tell him once he was medically in the clear. I dreaded this conversation more than any conversation I had ever had in my entire life. The afternoon we found out about Jackson's spinal cord injury, Alex asked me point blank if Jackson was paralyzed. There was no way for him to know this. He wasn't even in the same hospital as his brothers, nor did anyone from the other hospital ever visit him except for one time. I had asked my mother-in-law and husband's aunt Natalie to stay with Alex for about an hour so that I could be there when Jackson was taken back into surgery a few days before. Alex had spent the entire time begging them to be honest with him and tell him what was wrong with Jackson.

Once again, Alex was pleading with me to be honest with him and tell him what was wrong with Jackson. All I could say was "Yes." The despair I saw reflected from his eyes almost brought me to my knees. It would be a few days before we would have a "come to Jesus" talk, as I like to call it.

Alex continued to have severe panic attacks. Severe enough that he needed to be heavily sedated and had to take strong anxiety medicine at all times. As I was sitting with him in his step-down trauma room, he asked me a question about Jackson's diagnosis, wanting a specific answer. I told him we had plenty of time to discuss it later, as I usually did. I kept thinking that he needed more time to process it before we discussed what it meant long term for Jackson to be paralyzed. He looked me square in the face and said, "No. It isn't going to go away, and I *have* to talk about."

I calmly walked over to the door and shut it. We then proceeded to have a screaming match. I was finally able to get through to him by making him understand that his vehicle hydroplaned and there was absolutely nothing he could have done differently. I would scream at him, "If a car hydroplanes, who is in control of the vehicle?" He would answer, "No one." I would then scream, "And if no one is control of the car, who's at fault for the wreck?" He would scream back at me, "No one!" We repeated this over and over until our voices were hoarse. Before it was over, a nurse came to investigate, and I calmly asked her to leave the room. His father was next, and I simply pointed my finger to the door and said, "Go." By the time it was over, we were both depleted and spent, but in that moment, Alex finally started to heal.

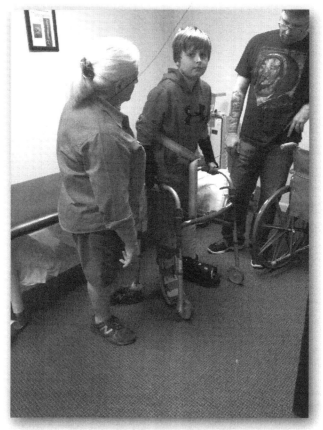

Jacob Walking for the First Time

August 28, 2015 (Facebook post)

I put makeup on today. Just a little, to feel human again. It seemed like such an insignificant thing before the accident. The smallest things in life I took for granted. Until something like this happens, we really cannot comprehend how precious our lives are, no matter the circumstances we are in. You always try to remind yourself on bad days to be thankful for what you have, but emotions rule in that moment. I was definitely a glass half empty kind of girl. I pray that I never again take a moment for granted. And I pray that if any of you are having a bad day, that you can find comfort in knowing it could be worse. It's not just something people say to make you feel better. Live today in the moment, knowing God is in complete control of whatever situation you're in. He's got this, so hand it all over to Him.

I was sitting on my thinking bench, as I liked to call it. It was a bench that was located right outside of Vanderbilt Children's Hospital. Sleeping was difficult for me, so I spent as much time as I was able sitting on that bench, praying and thinking. I love the outdoors and sometimes I felt as if I were suffocating in the waiting rooms. I decided that I was going to stop posting so much on Facebook and asking people to pray every day. I didn't want people to think that I was flooding their news feed with nothing but sadness, nor did I want anyone to think that I was seeking attention. It's funny when we think we have it all figured out but then God steps in and says, "Change of plans." God immediately put me in my place. He told me that my Facebook posts were not for me. They were to glorify Him and everything that He was doing for our family.

That very same day, I received an e-mail from a woman who told me she had lost someone she loved and had struggled to forgive God for over twenty years. Because of our story, she had learned to forgive and had started to attend church again. The e-mails started flooding in. People began to forgive others, forgive God, reconnect with Christ, and were saved. By watching through Facebook what God was doing for our boys, they knew there had to be a God and asked Him into their hearts. I still remind my boys of this today. Their lives and everything they went through impacted thousands of other people's lives. It was never just about them.

The devil also tried to use my Facebook posts, but in a negative way. I quickly learned that if I posted about a miracle that God had done, the devil would do everything he could to cause me to question or doubt it. I had to really learn to stand on faith. There were times when I would think, "I should wait to post this, just in case." In case of what? For God to change His mind? The devil tried to instill fear in me. He wanted to shut me up. The devil didn't want me to talk publicly about God. It would be in the form of a bad test result or the doctor delivering bad news after we were told that they were in the all clear. But the thing is, God doesn't change His mind. He doesn't take back what He has promised. His word is final, and what He commands, so shall it be. Nothing the devil could do was going to change that fact. This was another way that God helped me grow in my faith. Everything—yes, everything—works together for good for those who love Him (Romans 8:29). Even in the midst of crisis, God is there with us. He is trying to teach us and help us grow. We just have to be open to hear what He is saying. And every single time, the devil was a liar. God would show up and contradict those bad test results, or the doctor would apologize for reading the tests wrong. I cannot tell you how many times over the course of the next few months this would happen. I would just smile and say, "It is all because of Him."

I had front-row seats to watch God work. Sometimes when we pray, we don't always see results immediately. I have thought many times, in hindsight, that God had indeed answered a prayer of mine and I had not realized it. Therefore, I never thanked Him for the answered prayer. These prayers, by thousands of people, were answered immediately. And in ways that was undeniably God. We would be told that one of the boys would need surgery, and in the process of scheduling it, the doctor would come back and say that actually, surgery was not needed. The x-rays had been read incorrectly. Situations like this happened time and again.

—⚭—

> After I first woke up from Heaven, I opened my eyes
> to see a man standing over me. I was being rolled on
> a stretcher or carried. I am not sure which.
>
> Jackson

—⚭—

August 28, 2015 (Facebook post)
The NICU made an exception to allow Itsy to see Jackson. She did so well the nurses told me to have her registered as a therapeutic dog! Jackson and Alex both loved it and so did she! She knew where they were hurt and was so careful with them. Needless to say, after two weeks I was in Heaven

holding her again! A huge THANK YOU to Amber Whitley for taking care of my other baby and taking the time to bring her to Vanderbilt for a visit!

It is amazing how much I missed my long-haired Chihuahua Itsy through all of this. She had been with me every single day until the accident. She went to work with me. She traveled on vacations with our family. I missed her as I would have missed my child. Getting the chance to have visits with her was an absolute blessing. At first, the NICU told us that animals were not allowed. Once they realized how much she meant to the boys, they decided to make an exception. I will always be grateful to the nurse who made sure this could happen for Jackson. After we provided her immunization records, she was finally allowed to visit. When Jackson first saw her, his eyes simply lit up. She walked around his entire body without touching him, searching for his injuries. The entire time she was there, she never went near his broken arm. She stayed close by his other arm as he petted and loved on her. She was also able to visit Alex, and she did the same exact thing: identified his injuries first. She sniffed all his injuries and made sure to only get near the leg and arm that weren't injured. Animals are an important part of what makes up a family, and we truly love all our fur babies.

August 29, 2015 (Facebook post)

Even though I suck at video games, I loved getting to play the Wii with Jackson! I hope he feels up to more game time today and that he gets to finally eat a cherry popsicle! Please continue to pray that the infection leaves his body and pray for us parents as we have taken on a more active role in medical decisions.

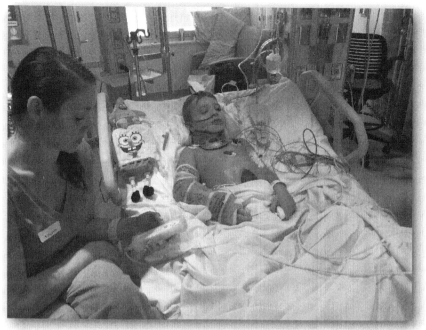

C.C. Playing the Wii with Jackson

Until this point, the doctors told us what needed to be done, and we signed whatever it was that needed to be signed. We knew instinctively that every surgery was necessary to keep Alex and Jackson alive. We had complete and absolute trust in the decisions of both of their doctors. Slowly, a shift started to occur. During one of Jackson's surgeries on his stomach, his vitals dropped, and they had to quickly close him up. We discovered later that his blood count was too low. My husband had noticed the evening before the surgery that he was pale and showing signs of a low blood count, so he mentioned it to the doctor. We assumed that they had checked it prior to surgery but later discovered they had not.

It was at this point that we decided to take an active role in his medical decisions. We still had complete faith in his medical team, but we also realized that as his parents, we knew our children better than anyone. It was a great place to be in, because it meant that he was healing enough that we had time to contemplate an action plan for his care. It was also very scary. Instead of just signing the papers, we started asking questions. We also started offering alternatives, such as doing the surgery without sedation and instead doing it with only pain medication. We knew by this point he couldn't feel anything below his chest, so there was no need to completely sedate him. Jackson was literally the best patient a doctor could ask for. He did everything they asked of him, without complaint. When I say he is the bravest kid I have ever met, I mean it unequivocally and absolutely.

The only thing that Jackson was afraid of was needles. We asked doctors to draw blood or run IVs through his foot. After all, he couldn't feel it there, and there was no reason to cause him pain by doing it in his arm. He didn't like to see it, so I would hold a blanket or pillow in front of his face and distract him. I also learned to ask doctors and nurses to not talk about what they were doing. It was natural for them to try to gently talk the patient through the process of what they were doing, but in Jackson's case, he simply didn't want to know. He wanted to tune them out and pretend that nothing was happening beyond our makeshift fort.

August 29, 2015 (Facebook post)

My brother's company spent the entire day building a ramp for our boys! They are coming back tomorrow to put handrails on. I am amazed at how many people want to help us and we want everyone to know it is so very much appreciated!

I am just as humbled today as I was then. Our community rallied around us in every single way possible. We received so many care packages that we provided snacks and drinks for our entire family as they took shifts with the boys. The packages contained everything from books, magazines, and necessities such as toothpaste and deodorant to snacks and drinks. I don't know what we would have done without these packages.

—※—

Angels have to earn their wings. I don't know if they do that while on earth or in Heaven. I just know they earn them.

Jackson

—※—

My husband and I never considered leaving the hospital until several weeks after the accident and only when we knew they were no longer in critical condition. We went to a local Target about five minutes from the hospital to grab necessities such as shampoo and deodorant. We probably looked like crazy people running through the aisles throwing items into the cart as quickly as possible. All we could think about was getting back to our boys as quickly as possible. Alex called my phone while we were there, and I literally played hot potato with my phone trying to answer it. While we were in line, another register opened, and a couple skipped line in front of us. I was thinking, "Don't they know our babies are in the hospital and we need to get back to them *now*?" I was beyond frustrated and stood in line fuming. As we waited, the person in front of them had to have a price check, and they ultimately had to wait anyway. We were checked out, and they were still standing there waiting.

Even then, God didn't let me gloat. He rebuked me and told me that I had no idea what was going on in their lives. They too could have a child in the NICU, possibly in worse condition than our boys were in. It wasn't my place to judge others. Everyone has a story. Each person has trials he or she must face, and I can't assume I know what the reason behind every action is. Talk about a lesson learned. I look at life's small inconveniences differently now. If someone cuts me off in traffic, I try to remember that that person may be rushing to be by the side of a dying loved one. Yes, someone could just be in a hurry to watch *Monday Night Football*. The fact is, I simply don't know and therefore will act with patience.

My husband and I were sitting on my thinking bench one night while he told me about a nurse who had told him how thankful she was that we stayed with our children and took active roles in their daily care. Well, of course we would! She explained to him that a lot of parents leave their children to the care of the nurses, sometimes all day. At first, I was absolutely horrified. Why would parents do this? How could they leave their children?

God once again stepped in to remind me that it isn't my place to judge others. Those parents leaving their children didn't have the support from a community as we did. Some of these children had reoccurring medical crises and spent weeks at a time in the hospital, sometimes several times a year. These parents still had to work to pay their bills. They didn't have any choice other than to leave their children in the care of the nurses.

I met so many parents on my thinking bench and had the chance to listen to their stories. Many of these parents were thousands of miles from home. They had spent months in the hospital watching while their children were fighting for their lives. My heart broke for each and every one of them. Because of the GoFundMe account, we were able to stay with our boys. It is very expensive living out of hospitals, as well as having children stay with separate family members. My husband and I were both self-employed, which meant that although we didn't have to worry about losing our jobs, we were not making the same amount of money we normally would have if we were there to manage our own businesses. We had bills from both of our businesses, as well as our personal home expenses, to cover. If people had not donated money to us, we would have lost everything. We were beyond blessed by the people who gave to our family so freely. Because of them, we didn't have to make the choice to leave our children.

I decided from that point forward that I would pray for those parents who didn't have the freedom that my husband and I had. I can only imagine how difficult it must have been for them.

At first, I believed that I had it worse than anyone else at the hospital. I had not one, not two, but four kids in the hospital all at once. But the truth was, I didn't have it worse. Every parent with a child in the hospital was going through the same heartache and fear that I was. We were afraid. We felt helpless not being able to help our children. We worried about our other children, our jobs, and how we would pay the medical bills that were quickly accumulating. We were all praying that God would heal our children and let them stay with us a little longer.

During Alex's first surgery, I was sitting in the waiting room watching the screen for his name to appear with an update. There were over a hundred people there, all waiting to hear about someone they loved. Some talked quietly with family. Some read books. Some slept in chairs. We all had one thing in common: someone we loved was in surgery. I was sitting there contemplating how bad I had it. I had one son in surgery in the adult hospital, one son in surgery in Vanderbilt Children's Hospital, and two other sons in regular hospital rooms. My oldest son was sitting beside me and worrying about medical issues that he too was facing. I was seriously feeling pitiful. Talk about having a pity party! I was desperately in the throes of one. "How could God possibly think I could handle this?" And then I overheard a father speaking with someone about his children. He was explaining that the only way to save the life of one of his children was for the other child to donate a vital organ, and the surgeon could not guarantee that the surgery would be successful. They were both currently in surgery. It is amazing how God can put things into perspective for us that quickly. It is not up to us to determine how much others are suffering or the trials they are going through. All we need to do is pray for them and love them in any way possible.

— ⚭ —

Trust in the Lord with all your heart: do
not depend on your own understanding.
Seek his will in all you do, and he will
show you which path to take.

PROVERBS 3:5—6 NLT

August 30, 2015 (Facebook post)

WE KNEW THE time would come when Jackson would finally start asking questions (because we had faith he would heal). My husband and I have spent countless hours deciding what to say when the time came. Last night he finally asked, "Why can't I move my legs?" Expecting the worse, we explain to him that he was in a wreck and had to have surgery on his tummy and back. His immediate response was to list all of the positives about being in a wheelchair: I get to have people push me around. I don't have to sit in a chair at the table when we go places to eat. Me and my brothers can play wheelchair bumper cars, just to name a few. His eyes lit up when he saw a picture of the wheelchair ramp (certainly thinking about flying down it in his wheelchair). How amazing is the human spirit that God gives our little children??? The world makes us negative, judgmental, and cynical. But God gives all of us a fresh canvas to begin with. I know there will be days ahead that Jackson will question why. When he is being pushed beyond measure to do what he doesn't think his body can do. But I pray that God protects his spirit. That *our positive happy go lucky kid continues to thrive despite his circumstances. As parents, we will do everything we can to heal his body, mind, and spirit.*

This would be the first of many conversations we would have with Jackson after the accident concerning his spinal cord injury. He understood that he wouldn't walk again, but we were still careful about what we said around him. We never wanted to give him the idea that it was completely hopeless. It was imperative that he have an overcoming spirit versus defeated one. It would be a couple of weeks later before he heard the word "paralyzed" associated with him, and it was completely by accident.

—◇—

Jesus showed me a wheelchair in Heaven, and I knew
that I would be in one when I got back to earth.

Jackson

—◇—

We broke records at Vanderbilt for having the most children LifeFlighted in critical condition at one time. Because the accident was so horrific and involved so many children from the same family, our story was featured on several local news stations. Because we knew how much people wanted to hear about how the boys were doing, we did several interviews over the first month. All the boys were excited to see the interviews, and some of the boys were in the segments. They thought it was totally cool to be on TV. Three boys were home with me during a follow-up story about our life at home while still being separated as a family, while my husband was at Vanderbilt with Jackson. The interviewer asked me about Jackson's injuries, and I told him about his paralysis. It was a small portion of the interview, but of course that ended up being the focal point of the entire interview that aired on TV. After the interview went off, Jackson became very quiet. After a few minutes had passed, he looked at his father and said, "You didn't tell me I was paralyzed." Even though he knew he couldn't move his legs or would never walk again, he hadn't associated it with the word "paralyzed." Words can have a huge impact on how people perceive themselves. Our fear was that Jackson would hear the word "paralyzed" and believe there was no hope. There is always hope when our faith is in God.

September 1, 2016 (Facebook post)

When I am not running between buildings, I take a moment to sit on a bench outside. This squirrel and I have become fast friends. Technically, he is friends with anyone that has food, but I'm okay with that! As I sit here, I think about the people who have reached out to me to tell me what an inspiration I am to them. My husband and I don't feel like we have done anything special. We are just doing what any parent would do. If you had asked me before the accident if I would still be standing on the Word of God in a situation like this, my answer would be a resounding NO! Not because I wouldn't want to be, but because I thought of myself as weak. So how can I be so positive? When you get to the scene of an accident and four of your children are pinned in the car and you hear them screaming, the only option you have as a mother is to hit your knees and pray. When a doctor looks at you and tells you the unthinkable, all you have left is to stand on His Word. As parents, we stick by our children's side. We love them, comfort them, and do our best to protect them. But at the end of the day, it is God who is in control. He is my strength above all else. My motivation comes from Him and our boys. From my oldest son, who comforted and took care of his brothers when his body was broken. Who had the wisdom to pray instead of giving in to fear. Who only screamed to yell, "Please get my brothers out of this car." I am inspired by my youngest son, who only saw the positive in this horrible situation. Who still smiles and never asks why. They are the true heroes and my inspiration!

September 3, 2015 (Facebook post)

Say a prayer today that Jackson's fever goes back down. He had such a great day yesterday and we want to continue having great days! Alex was given permission to start walking, but still unable to use his arm so pray that he can overcome this obstacle. Also pray for our boys at home who are still healing and separated from their brothers and for Justin Maston, who is taking care of our home while preparing to travel to Japan in a couple of weeks. We love all of you and couldn't do this without your prayers and words of encouragement!

Our oldest son, Justin, has always been fascinated by the Japanese culture. Justin's grandfather was in the military, so his father spent most of his youth stationed in Japan. He shared his love of Japan and the Japanese culture with his son. Justin decided to major in Japanese at Middle Tennessee State University, and we had been planning for over a year for him to study abroad in Japan. I was so excited for him to have the opportunity to live his dream, and I encouraged him in every way possible to go. Then the wreck happened. He offered to stay home and help with the care of the boys, and a very small part of me wanted to jump on his offer and keep him home, safe with me. We weren't even together as a family yet, and here I was planning to say good-bye to my firstborn son. But I wanted what was best for my son, and that meant putting him on an airplane knowing I wouldn't see be able him for an entire year.

C.C. and Justin

The night before Justin left, we stayed at Alex's father's house, as it was closest to the airport and Vanderbilt Children's Hospital. Some people would find it crazy that my husband and I would stay at my ex-husband's home. For us, it wasn't crazy at all. When Alex's father and I divorced, we decided to put our differences aside and coparent Alex to the best of our ability. He was our priority. He would come first, no matter what. We would make decisions as a team and do our best to provide not one, but two loving homes. We were not perfect and there were plenty of times when we would disagree, but we always eventually came to a mutual decision. Plus, I simply adored my ex-husband's wife. She loved my son, so how could I not love her? She was there for every baseball and football game. We all sat together to cheer him on, and I looked forward to those Friday nights. Her and Alex's relationship wasn't perfect. Alex tried everything he could to push her away during the early years, but I supported her in every way that I could. I am sure she has done the same for me by supporting my decisions over the years as well. After the accident, she was there holding my hand. She took turns staying by his bedside. Alex will tell you that he was lucky enough to be loved by two moms. All blended families cannot coexist in this way, but it is a blessing when they can.

The next morning, my husband said good-bye to Justin and headed back to Vanderbilt Children's Hospital to be with Jackson, while Alex and I headed to the airport to drop Justin off for his flight. Alex still couldn't walk very well, but he wanted to be there to say good-bye to his brother. It was the hardest good-bye I have ever made. The circumstances sucked. The accident had happened only three weeks prior, and I was still an emotional mess. I wanted to cling to him for dear life. He had been my leaning post through all of this. He was my sounding board. He was my only support system. Mostly, he was my best friend. Alex and I both cried leaving the airport. By the time we got to the hospital to be with Jackson, we had gotten ourselves together and put smiles on our faces.

C.C. and Alex's Stepmom Kyla at Graduation

September 3, 2015 (Facebook post)
We were finally able to see the car today. I am simply in awe of the Grace of God. My children should not be alive. Yet, they all still live and breathe! How amazing is our God?! My kids are broken physically, but their spirits are stronger than ever! Wonder if God exists? Simply look at these pictures...

The Front Side Passenger Seat Where Jacob Was Sitting

Side Image of the Car

Looking back on it, it seems so silly, but I did not want to see this car. I had such trepidation all the way to the Tennessee Highway Patrol, where the vehicle was stored. The only reason I went was because I wanted to get the boys' personal items, such as their school book bags and electronics. Both my husband and I had to sign for the release of the vehicle, so I had to be there. My heart raced as we followed the police officer back to the holding pen. As I saw the car, my heart shattered. I had known it would be hard to see. I knew the physical damage this vehicle had caused my boys' bodies. But what I didn't expect to see was the hand of God. I couldn't imagine any way for my children to be alive other than God declaring it so. I couldn't believe that Jacob had survived the accident and was the first one discharged from the hospital. The engine was literally sitting in the passenger seat, exactly where he had been sitting. There was no place for his legs to have been without every single bone in them getting crushed. Yes, he did have several broken bones, but he shouldn't have legs at all.

I stood beside this car and thanked Jesus for being there with my kids. I was overwhelmed with gratitude and thankfulness. The police officer who took us back was amazed that everyone had survived the accident. All I could say was, "It was only because Jesus was with them." We still have the vehicle that I was once so afraid to see. It is a reminder of how good God is. People who see it are simply amazed that they all lived. To see it is to know that there is a God, and He is still in the miracle business. The car that I was once so afraid to see now brings me comfort. Yes, I remember the pain and heartbreak of that day. The course that one simple moment in time set our lives on. But I am more reminded of the mercy and grace God bestowed on our family. No matter what the circumstances look like, God is bigger. You see that car and think there is no way, but God says, "Yes, there is always a way!"

September 4, 2015 (Facebook post)

We went to get the boys' electronics out of the vehicle yesterday. Alex wanted to give his iPhone 6 to Jackson. You should have seen the smile on his face when we gave it to him! I am amazed at the generosity and perseverance of our boys. It is humbling as a parent to realize how much I have yet to learn and can be taught by our kids. A trauma survivor came to visit Alex yesterday and told us the year of his accident was the best year of his life. It seems like such an odd statement to anyone who has never been through an experience such as this, but it is so true. If you open your eyes to what

God is showing you, you will discover just how blessed you truly are, in any situation!

Until you know trauma on this level, it is hard to understand such a strange statement—"best year of my life." I have always had a heart for these stories I saw on the news or social media or heard about from friends. I made a conscious decision not to watch the news simply because my heart would grieve too much for these unknown people who were going through so much. I couldn't imagine anything good coming from these stories. Looking from the outside in, I wouldn't have been able to imagine any good coming from having four children LifeFlighted to the hospital. From having a son who would have to learn to walk again and one who would never be able to do the things that he once could. A son who would have to fight for his life, go through surgery after surgery, and be paralyzed for the rest of his life. What good could come from such a tragedy?

We've all heard how intensive a Navy SEAL's training is. They literally break your body and mind through the training process. Only the strongest of the strongest survive. When it is over, these men and women become family for life. They are bonded together as a whole. That is the way I think about our experience. We learned more than we could have ever imagined about ourselves while living through this experience. We hit rock bottom as individuals and as a family. As parents, there was no place to be other than on our knees begging for God to step in and heal our children. We learned humility. Our pride was shattered. We depended on our family and friends. We needed support and prayers from people who had never met us but gave willingly and freely. Our family too was bonded, just like those Navy SEALs.

Our boys had to face more than most people could ever begin to imagine, at such young ages. They would have to overcome emotional and physical trauma. We all had personal choices to make. Would we become bitter and angry? Would we resent God for the pain we would endure, or would we praise Him for helping us to overcome? Alex had a choice: he could learn to forgive himself or live the rest of his life mired down in guilt, believing he was at fault for the accident. Jackson had a choice to make: to accept his diagnosis and learn to live his life despite being in a wheelchair, or become depressed and angry because he would never walk again. As the trauma survivor told me, "It can be the worst year of your life, or the best. It is your choice how you choose to walk away from this experience."

—⚏—

CHAPTER 7

God blesses those who patiently endure
testing and temptation. Afterward they will
receive the crown of life that God
has promised to those who love him.

JAMES *1:12 NLT*

September 5, 2015 (Facebook post)
MY VERY PERSUASIVE *son, Alex Arroyo, has persuaded the doctor to let him go home from Vanderbilt Stallworth Rehabilitation Center today instead of Tuesday. I am so happy for him and our other boys who can finally come home, but it is a little bittersweet for me as I will be leaving Jackson and my husband. Please pray for a safe trip home and for us parents, who now start the next phase of our journey separated.*

I knew how badly Alex wanted to go home. He thought that if he could only go home, he would feel better. I had no idea that my son could be so persuasive as to convince his doctor that he was ready to go home a week early. Of course, he wasn't ready, which he soon discovered. But sometimes the only way to learn something is to learn it the hard way.

My husband and I had known this day was coming. We would not only be separated by buildings; we would now be separated by cities. My heart ached because I wouldn't be able to see Jackson every day. Every couple of days, Alex would go to his father's so that I could visit Jackson and my husband, but it wasn't the same as being able to be with them every day. Being away from them every day was incredibly hard for me.

Leaving the hospital with Alex was extremely intimidating to me. I would have to change his dressings on his leg and arm. I would become the full-time caregiver for him. "What will happen if he falls? How will I transfer him from his wheelchair to the bathroom?" I remember how I felt when I had my first son and they were letting me leave with this beautiful newborn child. I thought, "Are they seriously going to let me leave this hospital with him? What are these nurses thinking? Do they realize I have never had a child before?" That was exactly how I felt when they let me leave the hospital with Alex.

September 6, 2015 (Facebook post)

We made it through our first night at home! It was an emotional experience for me. I hadn't had the chance to process the change to our lives until I walked into our home. We were redoing the boy's bedroom as a surprise the day of the accident. Alex was on his way home with them for the big reveal. I don't think it was a coincidence that I chose a chalkboard frame that says courage for their room. We have all had to have a healthy dose of courage through this and will continue to have to be strong for each other. Please continue to pray for our family. Our journey isn't over and we still need them, and in some ways, now more than ever.

After getting Alex home, I had to go to the pharmacy for his medicine. He was in too much pain from the hour-long drive from Vanderbilt to go with me, so Alex's father stayed with him while I went. I had to wait for his medicine because there were insurance issues and they were incredibly busy. It was my first time away from him and the first time I was back in my hometown. I rushed through the aisles getting things that I knew we would need, such as milk and bread, since we hadn't been home in weeks. My mother-in-law had traveled thirty minutes one way every other day to feed our cats and had told me that they would need more food soon, so I also grabbed cat food while I was there. Right in the middle of the pharmacy at seven o'clock at night, the reality of what we had been through and still had to go through finally hit me. I lost my breath. I couldn't believe that this was my life. Here I was, standing in the middle of our hometown pharmacy, waiting for a plethora of medicines for my son whom I had almost lost. I was an hour away from Jackson and wouldn't be there to tell him good night. Life is funny that way. We think we are handling things so well, and then bam! Reality sneaks in to hit us in our face.

September 6, 2015 (Facebook post)
(P.J.)
Jackson said he wanted to bust out of this joint. We just miss our family.

The separation was just as hard on my husband. Although we had been technically separated from each other the entire time, there were nights I was able to stay with him and Jackson. I could travel between hospitals and spend time with them. This was just the beginning of what would be a couple of months of being separated from one another.

September 7, 2015 (Facebook post)
I slept through the night only waking up once. This is a first since the accident. As a mother, I know I need rest. There comes a point after such a life changing event that life moves on to a new normal. It happens in phases. While living at the hospital we had different levels of routine. First you sleep in chairs and floors, then you move up to a cot in an actual room. There also comes guilt. My husband and baby are still at the hospital, while I must be home. Logically, I know I shouldn't feel this way, but I think it too is part of the process. I have found through this that I have learned so many life altering lessons. That is the point of grief. We all experience it in our lives to some degree. At the end of the journey, the true test is to be able to say that life does goes on and I have learned to be a better person despite it all.

—∞—

When I was in Heaven, there was no pain or sadness. Only love.

Jackson

—∞—

September 8, 2015 (Facebook post)
Several people have asked me who took the picture during the wreck that was posted on Facebook. The answer is simple. I did. My son had the bystander call me so he could tell me what happened. He calmly listed the boy's injuries as much he was could see. We were able to arrive within minutes of the paramedics and first response team. It may seem odd to some that I took a picture to post on Facebook when my babies were trapped inside a vehicle. The truth

is, I knew I needed fast and immediate prayers and Facebook was the fastest means available to me. After taking this picture, I knelt in the grass by the woman who had enough wisdom to be praying. I say all of this to remind everyone how much it has meant to us to have all of you follow our boy's recovery. You have been a part of our journey since the very first moment. Your words of encouragement and prayers have sustained us through this. Please continue to pray for us as we still have a long road ahead!

September 8, 2015 (Facebook post)
Urgent Prayer Request: The CT scan revealed another pocket in Jackson's tummy, which is why his fever has been spiking. He is scheduled to have surgery again tomorrow. Please believe with me that this will be the last surgery and that they remove all the infection this time! We are ready for his breakthrough and complete healing!

September 9, 2015 (Facebook post)
Another prayer answered! Jackson is out of surgery and doing wonderful! They were able to drain the fluid and he didn't even need a wound vac. Thank you all for your prayers. God is so good!

Fortunately, this would be Jackson's last surgery for a while. He would have to have two more surgeries much later, to repair the hernias the doctors had created to allow his wounds to heal. But this was finally the beginning of the healing process. This surgery finally cleared all the infection from his body.

September 11, 2015 (Facebook post)
I am disappointed that I can't go to Vanderbilt tonight to see my husband and Jackson because of the rain, yet I am so grateful that I get the chance

tomorrow. I was so close to never having that chance again. I cannot wait to see his smiling face in the morning. I am seriously blessed beyond measure!

Alex had to be sedated for the ride home from Vanderbilt Stallworth. I knew that it would be difficult for him. This was the first glimpse into how difficult it would be for Alex to drive in the future, especially in the rain. To this day, he has to work to overcome his fear of driving. I too have had my own fears of him driving and have to work through it. I know that he is a safe driver. He always has been. However, I now know that even when you do everything right, accidents still happen.

September 13, 2015 (Facebook post)

I will first start with a praise report…Yesterday was a great day for our boys. Justin had the chance to go watch his favorite team play his alma mater. Josh got to watch Vanderbilt play. Jacob and Jackson had a great time hanging out. Alex was able to watch his sister cheer. My husband and I even had a couple of hours to have lunch with each other that didn't involve cafeteria food! Now for the prayer request: The doctors discovered an infection in Jackson's blood. This means his stay at Vanderbilt will continue and he is unable to go to Atlanta. So please pray that the doctors are able to quickly identify the bacteria and treat it. He has been through so much and deserves a breakthrough. Thank you to everyone who continues to follow our boys progress and for keeping them in your prayers!

The devil comes to steal, kill, and destroy. He wants us to live in a place of fear. To think that God isn't big enough to overcome the battles we are facing. He wants us to think that no matter how far we get ahead, he will always find a way to push us back down. I used to think that in life you reap what you sow. Everything was a consequence to what you had done, and whatever hardship you were facing was in direct correlation to some sin that you had done in the past. As I learned to trust God and have a deeper understanding of Him, I realized that this simply was not the truth. Little children are not stricken with cancer because of something their parents did. People did not die in the World Trade Center because they had lived horrible lives full of sin. The truth is, God doesn't say that our lives will be free of troubles. In fact, the opposite is true. He warns us that we will go through trials and tribulations. The word tells us this is when we need to draw closer to Him. He comforts us by telling us in His word that he will never leave or forsake us (Deuteronomy 31:6). His own disciples were put through unspeakable trials in His name. Life isn't supposed to be all peaches and cream. We will face hard times. We will have moments of doubt. We will feel alone and scared. Sometimes, that light at the end of the tunnel just doesn't seem worth the effort it takes to get there. Even then, He is with us. Even then, He is waiting with His arms open wide, waiting for our embrace. There were moments after the accident that I cried out to God, "Why is this happening? It isn't their fault. They are innocent. Please, just make their pain go away!" He gently reminded me in the quiet moments that this was our journey to travel. Every single one of us was becoming stronger than we were before. We were all learning and growing through this together. The devil was going to attack in every way possible. He would try to steal God's glory. I only had to trust that God was in control. That He would be the victor. I had to stay strong and not let the devil win, because this was a fight to the finish line.

September 13, 2015 (Facebook post)

Joshua is insecure about the scar on his face from the wreck, but I believe he is even more beautiful than before! He looks brave and tough now. Plus, it highlights his dimple even more!

As parents, we are all faced with these life-changing moments in our children's lives. We know that how we react to the situation they are facing will define how they ultimately react for the rest of their lives. It is an opportunity to teach them a life lesson that will define who they are as a person. We don't always hit the nail on the head. Sometimes the child is simply too stubborn and refuses to listen. But the Bible tells us that eventually, if we train them in the way they should go, they will find their way back to it. I knew that this was one such moment in Joshua's life. I had been preparing myself for it. Each had his own battles to face after the accident, his own fears to overcome. And Josh's scar was his. After he finally had the courage to mention how insecure it made him feel, we started telling him how cool his scar made him look. We told him repeatedly that his scar showed the world what he had been through and had been able to overcome. Not many people had the chance to live through what he did and come out stronger than before. I told him how handsome and tough it made him look, and it even highlighted his dimple. See, I couldn't make that scar go away. But I could teach him to look at something that he felt made him different and instead see it in a positive way. We all carry scars, either on the outside or the inside. But what matters at the end of the day is whether we let those scars change us in a negative way or a positive way. It is not the action that defines us, but the reaction. And you know what? After the one-year mark, we let Joshua decide whether he wanted to have plastic surgery to reduce the appearance of the scar. He decided to keep it. He always wanted to see the reminder of what God had pulled him through. Yes, this mom allowed herself a pat on the back!

Joshua Attending the Vanderbilt Game and First Day Back at School

September 13, 2015 (Facebook post)

Alex has a hard time dealing with the wreck and worrying about his brothers. Today he made a huge leap and decided to visit Jackson for the first time since the accident. It was great to see them laugh and play the Wii together! I know I keep saying this, but seriously, could my kids be any more amazing?!?! So, yesterday I asked for prayers for Jackson because the doctors told us he had a blood infection. This morning they came in and apologized for misreading the lab results. He does have an infection, but not in his blood AND they have already identified the bacteria and are treating it.

Accident? I think not! I believe with all my heart that God is answering all of OUR prayers! Keep them coming!!

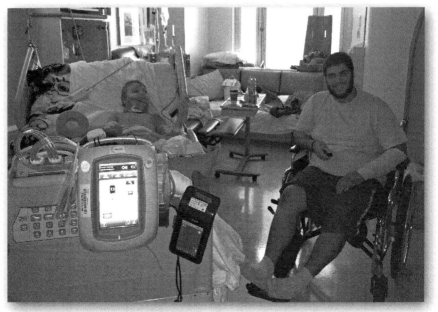

Alex and Jackson's First Visit After The Accident

Remember how I said the devil comes to steal, kill, and destroy? He wanted us to be in fear. To cower down. Instead, God used this as another opportunity to show that He was in control all along. This would happen again and again, and what the devil was really trying to do was shut me up. He didn't want me to share my praise reports. But more on that a little later.

September 15, 2015 (Facebook post)

Of course I have a praise report, because God is good! Jackson broke his fever last night and it hasn't come back! Today, they removed the pic line, which is a huge step toward getting him to Atlanta. They also replaced his cast with a new glow in the dark cast that allows him more mobility with his elbow and fingers (which he loves). I am simply amazed by the power of prayer! God has blessed us beyond measure to allow us a front row seat to watch Him in action with our boys! Today we found out that Joshua may have a fractured palate. Believe with us that the oral surgeon tells us tomorrow that he does NOT! Alex goes to Vanderbilt tomorrow where we will learn if he is able to use his hand. Please continue to pray for all of our boys as they all still need them!

September 16, 2015 (Facebook post)

I have front row seats to watch God work miracles. I have witnessed time after time doctors, who are renowned in their field, change their diagnosis. And not just the small stuff. The BIG stuff! At one time, a doctor told us Jackson's spinal cord was severed, giving us no hope. A few hours later, it was not severed, but stretched. I have witnessed the power of prayer. Fevers that indicate another infection simply vanish. Surgeries required suddenly are no longer needed. I have been given peace and faith the size of mountains. Not after the fact, but from the very first moment I received the call that my babies were pinned in a car. I am not special. I don't deserve His grace. But I serve a God who thinks that I am. A God who loves each and every one of us. Even when we don't think we deserve mercy and grace, He does! No matter what you are going through in life, know that God loves you and thinks that you are special and worthy of His grace!

These Facebook posts were allowing the world to watch me grow as a mother, a woman, and especially as a Christian. I knew that from the very beginning, this was my purpose in all of this. I would have to become vulnerable for what felt like the whole world to see. This doesn't seem like a huge thing, but for me, it was. You must know a little more about my background and who I am to understand how difficult being vulnerable and so transparent was for me. I grew up in the projects, or "ghetto," as some like to call it, in downtown Nashville. I was bullied and sometimes beaten daily, because I was the only white kid other than my brother who rode the bus to school every day. My neighborhood was littered with drug dealers, drug needles, and crime on top of more crime. I was molested by my stepfather from the age of five, and this continued for many years. I would be molested by many more men by the time I was thirteen. My mother was a single mom who had lived through her own abuse and trauma as a child, and she just couldn't get out from under her own cloud of depression to properly parent me or protect me. Even though she was aware of the abuse, her fear allowed her to stay in an abusive marriage and to continue to allow her only daughter to be molested over and over again. She is my mother and I love her, but this put a lot of strain on our relationship. It took being saved to fully understand the depth of her pain and how it affected her decisions. Forgiveness is a hard thing to offer, especially when we have been hurt on that level, but it is the only way for true healing to take place. It took a long time and a lot of work on God's part for me to finally get it. Now, where I used to feel only anger and bitterness, my heart aches for all that she too had to go through.

By the time I was fifteen, I was sexually active, drinking with friends, and making bad decisions. By the time I was sixteen and a freshman in high school, I was pregnant with my first son. He changed my life in every possible way and was the best thing that could have ever happened to me. My love for him was stronger than anything I had previously experienced. I went from making straight Fs to As and Bs. I faced all the criticism that a teenage mother could face, because

I knew deep down inside my soul that I would do whatever it took to be a good mother for my son.

When I was a junior in high school, the principal brought me into his office because I had missed a week of school because my son was sick. He told me that I wouldn't be allowed to make up my work and that I needed to quit school and go work in a factory so that I could provide for my child. He had been told that several girls had been overheard talking about how awesome it was that I had a such a cute little baby boy, and he didn't want his students thinking that being a single mother was easy. He explained that I was popular and all the other girls looked up to me, so I was giving them the wrong example. The truth was, I sometimes struggled to stay awake during class. My friends knew how hard it was to work, go to school, do homework, and stay up all night with a crying baby. I wasn't going to parties and hanging out, because I didn't have a babysitter. The principal didn't know all of that, but it wouldn't have made a difference. He had already made his decision. Now, when I look back on it, he didn't have the authority to force me to leave school. I was bullied into believing what he said because he was in the position of power.

However, that was a defining moment in my life. I had learned to be strong, and I had earned my stubbornness like a war trophy. I would not allow this man to define my future and take away my education. He would not force me to work in a factory when I knew I was capable of so much more. So I immediately enrolled in a GED program; scored the third highest in the state, barely missing out on a full scholarship; and was a freshman in college by the time my classmates were seniors in high school.

I wore my pride like armor. It helped me get to where I am to-day, but being strong can also have a negative impact on your life. Stubbornness can be useful in some life situations, but it can also cause you to miss out on so many things in life. There are times when we simply must bend and change course. I earned my associate degree and ten years later decided to obtain my bachelor's degree. Not because it would allow me to make more money, but because I wanted my boys to see that even a single mom could get a college degree. They watched me work full time while still taking care of them and going to school. They saw me study and do homework every single night, yet I never missed a single baseball or football game.

It was hard, but today that son I had as a sixteen-year-old girl is a senior in college and has lived in Japan for a year to follow his own dreams. Upon graduation, he plans to pursue his master's degree. That makes every single struggle and every sleepless night more than worth any hardship I had to face.

So letting down my guard and showing the world that I was vulnera-ble was extremely difficult for me at times. I have been told hundreds, if not thousands, of times how thankful people were that they could walk our family's journey with us. They have said how encouraging it was for them, and sometimes something I said was exactly what they needed to hear because they too were struggling with things in their own lives. I was sent e-mail after e-mail from other mothers who told me that my faith had refueled theirs. One woman hadn't been able to forgive God after the death of her child many years ago. Through following our journey, her faith had been restored, and she was fi-nally able to learn to forgive. One woman wrote to me sharing that she hadn't been to church in years, but through my story she finally started attending church again and seeking God.

I learned that I am not alone in this world. There were other women, just like me, who were growing in their walk with God. Women who were struggling with situations that their children were facing. It would have been selfish of me not to share my story. I have been asked by so many people to write this book. It was for them that I decided to put myself out there, allowing the possibility of failure. Even if I can help only one single person, it will have all been worth it.

—⚭—

I didn't get to go into Heavens gates because my name was not written in the book. You have to die be-fore you name is written in the book.

Jackson

—⚭—

September 16, 2015 (Facebook post)
Today was a great day! Justin Maston and Alex Arroyo got to visit with Jackson and take him to Ben & Jerry's. Joshua does NOT have a fractured palate and gets to start school tomorrow! Alex will not be able to use his hand for another month but other than that the doctors were very happy with his progress. We are praying that Jacob gets at least one cast off at his next doctor appointment and that hopefully by next week Jackson will be headed to Atlanta. Everywhere

we go someone tells us they are following our boys' progress and praying for us. So, thank you to everyone who shares our updates and continues in prayer for us!

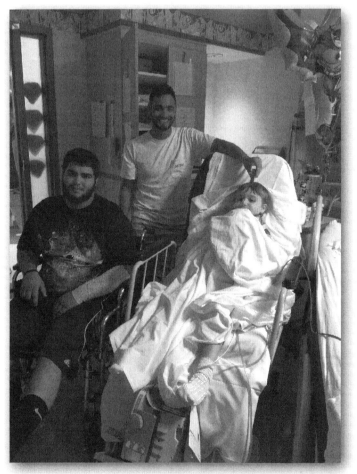

Justin Visiting His Brothers Before Leaving for Japan

September 17, 2015 (Facebook post)
Channel 5 did an in-home interview today and it will air tonight at six o'clock. Make sure to spread the word for everyone who wants updates on the boys!

The media was a huge instrument in our journey, and it helped spread the word for all that God had done for our family. It was also a painful learning experience. It was during this interview that that Jackson heard the word "paralyzed" for the first time. I felt as if the interview had gone great. They were there for Joshua's first day back at school. They were able to see our home, which was an extension of our family, and visit the room we had redone for the boys the day of the accident. I talked about how far we had come since that initial interview and how much God had done for our family. I got to tell them how thankful we were for all the volunteers who had donated their money and time to help our family get through such a difficult period. I was always so careful with the words I chose to use during these interviews because I knew that words had power. Only once during this interview did I even mention that Jackson was paralyzed with a complete T1 spinal cord injury, and I followed that by stating that God was the ultimate healer and our family didn't believe in the word "never." God had the ultimate say-so as to if and when Jackson would walk again. It was such a short part of the interview, yet somehow it became the entirety of the interview. I know it is all about adding to the emotional trauma for the segment and drawing viewers in. I knew from the very first interview that anything I said could be misconstrued and always strived to be careful with my words.

Unfortunately, all the boys were excited to watch the interview that evening on TV. Jackson was looking forward to seeing his brothers on TV, so he and his father counted down the hours and minutes until the interview came on in his hospital room. And from Jackson's room at Vanderbilt Children's Hospital, he heard me say on TV that he was paralyzed. He knew what that word meant. The power of one word can change a person's life. Although Jackson knew that he couldn't walk and that he had a spinal cord injury, he had never heard that word spoken aloud. He was aware that it was permanent. But the power of the word "paralyzed" hit him hard. The world "paralyzed" sounds so permanent and final.

He asked his father if it was true, and he had to tell him yes. He was quiet for a day or two after, letting the reality of that one word sink in. It changed his perception of his injury. Thankfully, we got Jackson through that, and even to this day, Jackson talks about the things he will do when he walks again. Yes, we all know that there is a high likelihood that he won't. We are not feeding him unnecessary hopes and dreams. But we chose from the very beginning to teach him to think about what could be. Many times, he has become upset because he was unable to do something. It is in those times that we teach him to think about what he can do or find a way he can make it happen. There is life and death in the power of the tongue, and the words that we choose to speak reflect what outcome we have. We choose to speak positive words. We choose to dwell on the possible, not the impossible.

September 18, 2015 (Facebook post)
Update: The doctors have told us to expect another two weeks at Vanderbilt before Jackson goes to Atlanta. This is actually good news. Up until this point they have not told us a date to work toward. God has this, we just have to wait on His timing!

Being an impatient person, I had to learn patience and learn it quickly. Nothing was in my control. Everything was in His. It was in God's timing, and all I could do was wait on Him. There is freedom in learning to be patient. It is freeing knowing that you are not actually the center of the universe and the world doesn't fit into your hands or do your bidding. I found comfort in knowing that He would take care of it, but only in His timing. I didn't want to rush their healing, and I didn't want to push them too far. God knew when things needed to happen, and it was according to His schedule alone, not mine.

September 19, 2015 (Facebook post)
(Ashley Greer)
"A wife of noble character who can find? She is worth far more than rubies…
she speaks with wisdom, and faithful instruction is on her tongue. Her chil-
dren arise and call her blessed; her husband also, and he praises her: many
women do noble things, but you surpass them all. Charm is deceptive, and
beauty is fleeting; but a woman who fears The Lord is to be praised." ~
Proverbs 31 You are a true Proverbs 31 woman C.C., thank you for your ex-
ample and encouragement to us all!

It was posts like this that reminded me why I needed to stay strong. It was because of friends and even perfect strangers that I made it through some of my hardest days. Although the world tries to teach us that we should answer to no one, there isn't anything wrong with being accountable to others. We are all accountable to God. It wasn't that I cared what others thought of me. I didn't live my life to impress others. It was just important to me that I was doing my very best for the thousands of people on social media who followed our family's story, but most importantly for God.

September 20, 2015 (Facebook post)
My son is on his way to Japan for an entire year. I am heartbroken and proud, all
at the same time. My heart is sad that I will not see him for such a long time. Yet,
I am proud that he is stepping out into the unknown to have an experience he has

always wanted. I am proud that I raised him to have courage and independence. The very best thing about a parent's life is the short stage in someone's story. And that is enough. Raising him has been the greatest wonder and privilege of my life. Selfhood begins with our children walking away. Love is watching them go, confident that you have taught them all they need to know to succeed. Please pray for this mom's broken heart and pray also for Justin to have safe travels.

No matter how much you prepare, you still lose a piece of your heart when a child leaves home for the first time. As much as I would worry about Justin while he was gone, I knew he had made the best decision for him. I was so proud of him for overcoming his fears. Although it was a hard transition for him at first, he ultimately would have a wonderful experience and fall in love with a beautiful girl named Aya (who I selfishly hope convinces him to live in the United States when they get married).

I was also proud of myself. When my boys were younger, my heart would grip in fear just thinking about being separated from them by so many miles. All of us moms go through this at some point. We think, "Who will take care of them if they get sick? Who will make sure they pay their bills and have groceries? How will I know if they are being responsible and doing the right thing?" Letting go is a part of life. It is the one thing we are guaranteed to have to do throughout our life: we send our children off to pursue their dreams, we lose a position or job that we were seeking, we lose our loved ones and must say good-bye forever. Over the next year or two, we would come to terms with so many things that our family had lost. Alex's freedom to be a normal high school senior. Both me and my husband's businesses and dreams. And most significantly, Jackson's ability to walk. No matter who we are, loss finds its way into our lives. It is inevitable and permanent. It is up to us how we choose to accept it and move on from it.

September 20, 2015 (Facebook post)
(P.J.)

It has been a long and exhausting five weeks. After seven surgeries and fighting fevers, I can say that Jackson is out of the woods and improving every day. He has fought for the will to live. Tomorrow they will remove his last wound vac. The doctor also said he will be released for rehab sometime this week. We will be there for four to six weeks. Now we can turn a page this week. I also want to thank everyone for the prayers and support. It has kept us strong as a family. Love you all.

September 21, 2015 (Facebook post)

Many of you praying have not had the pleasure of meeting Jackson personally so let me introduce you: I had the privilege of taking him to work with me every day before he started kindergarten as a stay-at-home mom and we both loved it! He still asks to skip school to go to work with me and paint all the time! He is the most carefree happy kid you will ever meet. He is incredibly smart, adores his brothers and knows how to put a smile on your face (even when you are supposed to be disciplining him). He is all boy and loves to run and play. I can count on two hands how many times he has thrown a full on temper tantrum (no, seriously!) He has a slight sarcastic side to him (he is his dad's mini me) and it tickles his nurses constantly. He looks at his father with such devotion and love it astounds me. My heart cannot see a future where he doesn't walk again. I simply can't imagine not seeing him run and play again. We are not naive. We hear what the doctors say. Yet we choose to believe that God will continue to heal him, as he has done this far. Jackson will take on this life sitting or standing, and totally ROCK it! Of that I have no doubt! But as a mom, I want to see him run and play again, as selfish as that may be. So, when you pray for him, pray that God works His wonders and heals him TOTALLY! Believe with us that Gods word is stronger and truer than any doctor's report!

Jackson

September 23, 2015 (Facebook post)

One last rose bloom (from my garden) before the season changes and it is a stunner! I am reminded that each season has its own beauty and wonder. I love summertime. Have never liked the fall or winter. Since the accident, I have learned to be thankful for every single day. I am blessed that my boys are here to enjoy the season change to fall, then winter. I look forward to the day they are ALL home and we can have campfires with s'mores, watch movies and eat chili. I will not even mind watching football constantly! I look forward to the day that the grass in front of the basketball goal is once again a dirt patch, because that will mean our boys are doing what they most love to do…playing ball together! Because this too is just a season in our lives and we will move on to another one, with all its own beauty and wonder.

CHAPTER 8

—⚬—

Faith is the assurance of things hoped for,
the conviction of things not seen.

HEBREWS *11:1 ESV*

September 24, 2015 (Facebook post)
LAST NIGHT JACKSON *got a visit from his brothers. Why?!? Because Jackson is on his way to Atlanta this morning!!! We are so excited for this next stage of our journey to begin! We have been told the average stay at Scottish Rite is six to eight weeks. Please continue to pray for healing for our boys and strength for us parents.*

As happy as were that Jackson had improved enough to go to Scottish Rite, it was also bittersweet. We would once again be separated, but this time there would be hundreds of miles and over four hours of travel time between us. Until this point, my husband and I had held on by a thread. The thread would slowly start to unravel at this point in our journey. Because Jackson would be permanently in a wheelchair, our home would have to have many modifications. At a minimum, we would need a wheelchair ramp, and some doors would need to be widened.

Many people offered resources, time, and help for these things to happen. Companies donated materials. But halfway during the remodel, which we were trying to have done before Jackson came home, a lot of people who had offered to help became busy with other projects. The person who had volunteered to manage the project was no longer able to do it. We understood, but this put a tremendous amount of stress on our family. When you widen doors, for example, you must also plan to purchase new door frames and hardware, redo flooring and transition pieces, repaint walls, and so on. So, we had a builder come in and cut walls to widen the doorways, but no one had offered to purchase the materials to do all the other things that would now have to be done. Imagine starting a remodel and getting halfway through, and then, suddenly, the contractor just walks away. That was exactly how this felt. We were basically trying to coordinate the remodel ourselves and begging people to help us finish it, while also funding a lot of the repairs.

It sounds tremendously negative, and I don't want to discredit all the people who gave freely of their time and money to help us accomplish this for Jackson. However, it is necessary for me to explain this so that you can understand the stress this put on our marriage. We alternated going back and forth to be with Jackson in Atlanta until it became clear I needed to be with Jackson more than I was needed at home. We all missed each other terribly. It was hard for the brothers to be separated from each other, and FaceTime only helped so much. Our youngest three boys were like three parts of a whole, and it just wasn't the same when one was missing. While I was home, my husband would become frustrated because he couldn't help with the construction. While I was at Scottish Rite with Jackson, my husband was having difficulty getting everything done that the boys needed to do while also working on the house. Every missed appointment made me that much angrier. I tend to be an overachiever and work myself into exhaustion. Men are not always the best at multitasking and managing schedules.

September 24, 2015 (Facebook post)

Prayer Warriors, we need you now! Jackson will be having a test in the next day or two to determine if he will ever walk again. Until now, his diagnosis was based only on the initial examination and the MRI. This is the time for God to show up and show out! Please pray for Jackson and spread the word as much as you can! We love all of you.

The anxiety we felt about this test was enormous. It would confirm or refute the MRI and what the doctors believed was true. At this point we still had little knowledge about spinal cord injuries. The only way I can explain it is to consider suddenly getting a life-altering diagnosis. You must learn how to live completely differently. You hear words that you have never heard spoken, and it sounds as if the doctors are speaking a foreign language. There were times when I felt embarrassed because I had to ask what something meant, but then I would remind myself that this was something that I had never expected to happen or had ever prepared for. No parent ever expects this to happen. You watch it in the movies, you see it on TV, and you hear about it happening to other people in the news, but you never consider that it can happen to you.

We knew Jackson was paralyzed, but until this point we didn't know whether he had a complete or incomplete injury. A complete spinal cord injury means that there is no feeling beneath the point of injury, or, in other words, the point where the spinal cord was stretched. An incomplete spinal cord injury means there is some feeling below the point of injury. We were hoping there would be some spinal cord matter still attached. I cannot state enough how thankful we were that Jackson's point of injury was below his arms so that he would be able to become completely self-sufficient someday. We just hoped that perhaps there was some feeling in his legs so that we would have a building block to build upon.

We had no idea what this test would entail, but we knew it was important. I was at home with the boys, so my husband was with Jackson at Scottish Rite during the first test. We expected some elaborate imaging test but realized that Jackson had already undergone this same test several times at Vanderbilt Children's Hospital. The best way to explain how they achieve results is that the doctor took a paper clip and used the pointy side and the curved side. They proceeded to ask him while they touched various places on his body with the paper clip if he could feel it, and if so, was the feeling sharp or dull? It really was just that simple. The test confirmed that Jackson had a complete T-1 spinal cord injury. This simple test confirmed the MRI and our worst fears. Before he left Scottish Rite, they performed the test again, confirming their original diagnosis. This was it. There would be no more tests and no more chances for hope. The only way Jackson would ever walk again was if science or God intervened. Even then, we still had plenty to be thankful for. Had Jackson's injury been even a few millimeters higher, he would have been a quadriplegic and unable to use his arms. When I think about how close it was, I am overwhelmed with gratefulness.

—៣—

From the very beginning, the guilt at not being able to be everywhere at once was staggering. We could only be in one place at one time, which meant we could be with only one of our boys at a time. Our circumstances were quite different from the norm. We didn't just have one child in critical condition, but four. I believe that is why so many people were able to connect with our story. They just couldn't fathom going through what our family was going through.

P.J., the boys' dad

—៣—

September 25, 2015 (Facebook post)
Jackson wanted Alex Arroyo to see that he could already roll himself in his wheelchair so he took this video for Alex to see him in action. He said Alex better step up his game! I just love my boys.

Boys by nature are competitive. They love to challenge one another to determine who is the fastest or the strongest or the smartest. This time was no different. They pushed each other and motivated each other. Alex and Jackson, from the very first moment, walked their journeys simultaneously. When one was sick, so was the other. When one had a fever, so do did the other. If one had to have surgery, so did the other. Although their injuries were completely different from each other's, they shared similar experiences. Both boys would continue to do so.

Jackson's First Time Outside After the Accident

September 27, 2015 (Facebook post)
We finally have 3 boys home together again! Jackson's test will be at 9am tomorrow morning so please continue to pray that we get great news! God has got this!

September 29, 2015 (Facebook post)

Jacob got his first real shower since the accident! It took about an hour to take all the boots off and wrap his cast, then another one to get him in the tub, but he thinks washing his hair was totally worth it! My back, however, isn't so sure!

As a family, we rejoiced with any small amount of progress, and any step forward was something to be celebrated. Having three of the boys home together was a huge blessing, but it also made us feel my husband's and Jackson's absence even more. It also increased the level of care whichever parent was at home had to be able to give. First, there was one child in a wheelchair, and then there were three. Each boy had doctors to visit and therapy appointments to go to. This meant trying to arrange schedules, which wasn't always easy to do. Suddenly, we were live-in nurses. We had to learn about medications, how to change wound dressings, and how to transport children with injuries. Every small task took a long time to prepare and plan for. A simple shower could take over an hour, and going to the bathroom was a huge ordeal. There were some nights when I would fall into bed exhausted. I think God gives us a small amount of supernatural strength to get through times like this because when I look back on it, I still don't know how I was able to do it, physically or emotionally.

Alex's First Time Outside After the Accident

September 28, 2015 (Facebook post)

I will start by saying that God has blessed us beyond measure. We know that He has a purpose and a plan in this situation. The second the car started to hydroplane, Alex heard God telling him to not be afraid because everyone and everything would be okay. This was before Alex even knew they would hit the other vehicle. Our mantra since day one has been as long as they still live and breathe, we can get through everything else. With that being said, the test showed that Jackson is paralyzed from the chest down. We knew this already, but prayed that today's test would show that some sensation could come back. Luckily for us, our hope is not in this test, but in God. We are also prepared for this to be His plan for Jackson's life. Even if Jackson never walks again, he will still have a great life. Jackson has shown more bravery than I have ever seen in my life. He is the most positive person you could ever be around. He will still do great things! Continue to pray for our family. We need strength in the days, weeks and months ahead. Please also pray that God provides for us financially as we will not be able to return to work for at least a couple more months. We also have to make our home and vehicles wheelchair accessible. Thank you to all who have prayed and have supported us since day one. Know that it has meant the world to us and helped get us through this! 1 Samuel 1:27–28

September 29, 2015 (Facebook post)
(Gina Ritter—Family Friend))
Okay friends, I need help! I'm sure many of you have seen on the news about the family out of Shelbyville who's four kids were in a near fatal car wreck. I had the honor of visiting with them today. I cannot express to you the goodness in this mother's heart. The doctors confirmed to them today that the six-year-old will be permanently paralyzed from chest down, the 18-yr. old will have more surgeries, one child just started school again today, and the other one is still home bound in a wheelchair. So, three of the four children are in wheelchairs, and one will remain in one the rest of his life. The problem… their home is NOT handicap friendly. The wheelchairs barely fit through the doors to go to the bed rooms or bathrooms, and the bathroom shower/tub will not allow them to be able to be wheeled in. Scotty and I will be ripping out the shower/tub combo and replacing it with a big shower, big enough to wheel those kiddos right in. The next problem…we specialize in cultured marble (showers, tubs, vanities, etc.), but we can't do the framing, or plumbing. We need a toilet to be moved, and we need door frames to be wider. Please, if you are in this type of business or know anyone who is, please ask them to help this family. The work would have to be done for free, as they have a lot of medical bills to be paid. The six-year-old that is paralyzed will be home from the

hospital in about 3 weeks, so we are trying to get this done asap. Please share my post so we can spread the word!! God bless!

Gina and her husband were such a blessing to our family. By this point we knew how desperately we needed to remodel the bathroom to accommodate Jackson. The other three boys were already home and in wheelchairs, and this helped us to see what would need to be done for Jackson long term. Scotty and Gina Ritter offered to completely remodel the bathroom to accommodate Jackson so that he could wheel himself into the shower and would be able to fit under the sink. They also agreed to help find vendors to help us finish the remodel that had already been started. Although Gina and I had been friends for several years, it still amazed me that people would go out of their way for us. It's not until something like this happens to your family that you realize just how much you mean to others. It allowed me to see that there is so much more good in the world than even I had ever realized. My once-cynical heart was beginning to rapidly thaw.

October 1, 2015 (Facebook post)
Jackson has always been an overcomer! This time two years ago he broke his leg in half on the playground at school. He had multiple surgeries to reset his leg and was confined to a wheelchair for almost 3 months. He didn't let it stop him from doing anything and I know beyond a shadow of a doubt that this won't be any different! #overcomer #godhasthis

October 1, 2015 (Facebook post)
(P.J.)
Jacks goal of his physical therapy session is to sit up unassisted for 3 minutes, so that is what he did. Needless to say, I am one proud dad.

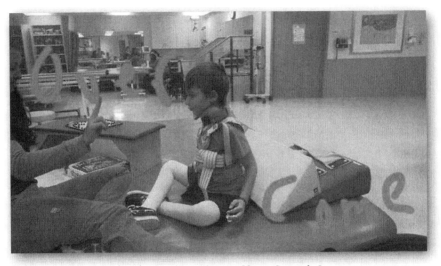

Jackson's First Time Sitting Up at Scottish Rite

I remember watching Jackson, after breaking his leg, crawl around the floor to get to wherever he wanted to go. He has always been the child who didn't see obstacles in his way. He just finds a way to bust through them or go around them. My husband and I have said many times that if this was going to happen to any of our children, Jackson would be the one to overcome it. Not necessarily that he would walk again, but that he wouldn't let it control his life. He wouldn't let something like a wheelchair slow him down or stop him from accomplishing what he wanted. It hurts to see any of your children in a wheelchair, but it is especially painful to see your baby in that position. Yet we knew with everything in us that Jackson would be okay. From the very beginning, every single goal that Jackson was given he tackled head on. To this day, he still has that same fighting spirit.

—∞—

Our family was covered in love and spiritual support from the very beginning. We were also thankful that so many gave in the way of monetary blessings, because without those, I don't know how our family would have made it through the next year. Early on, someone gave us $5,000 on the GoFundMe account. They didn't even attach their name or e-mail address to the donation for recognition. God made a way and used his angels here on earth; that is the only explanation.

P.J., the boys' dad

—∞—

October 2, 2015 (Facebook post)
(Niki Swanson—Family Friend)
C.C. Hasty Andrews, me and Ashley Nicole Hileman saw your Honda that the boys were in on our way home and all I can say is God is amazing. They had guardian angels looking out for them that day. It is truly amazing they made it out alive after seeing it in person. Wow! That's all that came out of my mouth. That's all that would come out of my mouth. It just shows that there is an amazing God watching over us.

October 4, 2015 (Facebook post)
It is amazing to see our story from the beginning to now. There is no doubt that God has been by our side since the very first moment. Although my heart aches sometimes for the pain that my boys have gone through and the things

that they have lost, I praise Him anyway, because I know that God is bigger than this. Our boys have touched so many people's lives and this is just the beginning! Jeremiah 17:14

October 6, 2015 (Facebook post)
(Tammy Quick—Family Friend)
I saw God at work through people today and it's all hitting me. Wow is all I can say. Amazing parents and amazing kids. Amazing awesome contributors. The people today forever will have impacted a very special family and very special little boy. C.C. and P.J., thank you for touching all of our lives.

October 7, 2015 (Facebook post)
We are so amazed at how many people have been willing to donate their time and money to help us get Jackson home! After the concrete was poured, we wrote, "For this child I have prayed, and the Lord has given me my petition which I asked of him. 1 Samuel 1:27." We wrote all the boy's names and the date August 19, 2015—which is the date Jackson lived through his surgery. We don't want to remember the date of the accident, but the date that God was faithful to His Word. A huge thank you to Tammy Quick and Gina M. Ritter for coordinating the "Bring Jackson Home" remodel!

October 8, 2015 (Facebook post)
(P.J.)
I was invited to a meeting today with other parents to talk about stress and how to cope with trauma that happens within a family after traumatic events. It was me and two other dads'. I'm not the type of person to just spill my emotions. In the last two months, there is a lot of them. As I sat and thought about it, "How did I get through this. How did I make the right decisions at

the emergency room? How was I even walking around? How did I look at my kids laying there on a table badly hurt? How did I even drive to the hospital while all my kids were being flown in a helicopter to Vanderbilt Children's Hospital?" I have been asked the question, "How did y'all do it" quite a few times. It was God. And then my wife, family and friends even on social media. Prayers, support from the community. I am a much stronger person today than I was on August 16. Being here with Jackson has taught me a lot about my faith in God and the love I have for my family. Jackson told me out of the blue last night that Jesus saved him and that has weighed heavily on my heart. I left it at that. Jackson Andrews has saved his first person and that's me!

This was the first time that Jackson had mentioned God after the accident. My husband and I discussed it and decided not to ask to him about it but instead to let him share when he was ready. This revelation from Jackson led my husband to accept Jesus Christ as his Lord and Savior. I knew from the very first moment that God was with them on the day of the accident. Alex had shared his experiences, and I somehow knew that Jackson too had also had an experience. Every time you walked into Jackson's room in the NICU at Vanderbilt Children's Hospital, a calming sensation would wash over you. It was almost as if he had brought a little piece of Heaven back with him. No matter how scared you were or how badly your heart hurt, being around Jackson was like a soothing balm. Over the course of the next two years, Jackson would slowly share his experience in Heaven with us, and boy, was it amazing!

October 13, 2015 (Facebook post)

I usually try to only post positive uplifting things. That is what mothers do. We try to mother not only our own, but everyone around us. Yesterday was emotionally trying for me. It is harder than most can comprehend to push your son when he is at his breaking point. But you do it anyway, when all you really want to do is cry and beg them to stop. You don't, because you know that it is what's best for him. It is in those moments when you want to scream at the world that this isn't fair! Why did this happen, and to all people Jackson?!? This sweet happy go lucky child who doesn't deserve this. You want to blame fate, yourself, God...anybody! That is when God shows up with His mercy and grace, to remind you that everything is according to His purpose and good. Life isn't fair, but He is. Situations that we are thrown into suck, but He has a plan. I can't take this away, make it better, or carry this cross that Jackson must burden, but He can. I am sharing this for all the mothers who feel like they must carry the burdens for their children too. Just know that it is okay to have a bad day. To feel abandoned and helpless. It is also okay to feel that life isn't fair. But know that God is in the midst of your circumstances and He is in control. He loves our children even more than we do, although that is hard to imagine. Trust in Him to carry you through the storm and cast your cares over to Him.

CHAPTER 9

The LORD hears his people when they call to him
for help. He rescues them from all their troubles.
The LORD is close to the brokenhearted, he
rescues those whose spirits are crushed.

PSALM 34:17–18 NLT

October 15, 2015 (Facebook post)

AFTER CONTEMPLATION AND a lot of prayer, I decided to share Jackson's experience on Facebook, with his permission. I wondered if it was my story to tell. How would people react to it? Would they be negative or judgmental? Then God reminded me over the last few days that this has been my part of our story since the very first moment I posted the picture of our kids trapped in the car on Facebook. Our story has seen countless people saved or renew their faith in God. After the accident, Jackson mentioned on several occasions that Jesus saved him. We never questioned this or pushed for an explanation. This week, during a normal walk from a trip to the game room, Jackson made a comment about how much easier it would be to be able to walk (he was not complaining, just stating a fact). I explained to him that God has a purpose and a plan for this happening to him. He told me, "I know, God could heal my whole body if He wanted to." I said, "Yes, but we have to wait for His timing." He then said, "I know, that's why Jesus saved me." I asked him what *he meant by that. He proceeded to tell me that on the day of the accident he saw Jesus and explained to me what He looked like. He told me that He was white with brown hair and had a white robe on. I asked him what color eyes He had and Jackson said, "I have no idea, I wasn't paying attention to his eyes!" I asked him if Jesus spoke with him and he said, "No, He didn't have to." I can only assume this means that Jesus didn't have to verbally speak to him. He explained his experience to me so matter-of-factly, as if it was no big deal. And to him, it wasn't. It happened and it is fact. I will not press him for details, nor do we want anyone else to do so. This is his story to ultimately tell. It is his testimony and we in no way want to convolute it or distort his memory of the incident. I decided to share it because I know that so many people have said, "God was with those boys" or something to that affect. The truth is, He was. In every way, shape or form. He spoke to Alex, He freed them from pain in the vehicle, He appeared in person to Jackson, and He has since performed miracle after miracle. There is no doubt in my mind that this happened for a reason. Our purpose is to continue to live our lives in a way that encourages and uplifts others. To share our story so that others may know that yes, there is a God. Yes, He does exist, and He is still present in our lives every single day. There is no reason to doubt, to be afraid, or live in fear. Some may say that Jackson is only seven-years-old. That he really didn't see Jesus. He told me about his experience while it was just the two of us. In such a matter of fact way that it leaves no room for doubt. I believe with my entire being that yes, he did indeed see Jesus on August 16, 2015, and someday Jackson will share his experience with the world.*

I remember the day Jackson first told me that he went to Heaven, as if it just happened yesterday. I was pushing his wheelchair from behind, so he had no way of knowing that I was actually behind him sobbing like a hysterical crazy person. As we passed people going down the hall at Scottish Rite, they gave me the oddest looks. I'm sure they thought I had finally lost it. I didn't care. The only thing I could focus on was putting one foot in front of the other and trying to keep the sound of tears from my voice as I talked with Jackson. I didn't want him to see me crying. I didn't want to scare him or make him feel afraid to speak with me about his story. I desperately wanted to ask him questions because I had a million of them swimming around in my head at once. "What did Heaven look like? How did you get there? Are there really angels? Did you see anyone you knew? How did you feel? Did you fly or walk?" As much as I wanted to ask these questions, it was more imperative that Jackson talk and I listen.

I've read stories about other children going to Heaven. I've watched movies. I've always been fascinated with them, and although I had no reason to doubt their stories, I wasn't personally there, nor did I personally know these families to know whether their story was true or not. And here I was, right in the middle of my own story. Jackson is my son, and I know when he's telling the truth or not. I was the one he decided to share his story with. I listened firsthand about Jackson's experience in Heaven, and I knew beyond a shadow of a doubt that he was telling the truth.

When I tell people of Jackson's visit to Heaven, no one laughs at me, ridicules me, or mocks me. The typical response is complete and absolute acceptance. People are excited to hear his story. Almost every single time, the listener will comment, "I believe it beyond a shadow of a doubt." I'm sure living right smack in the middle of the Bible Belt has helped with people's acceptance.

I am sure that at some point that may not be the case. I am prepared for someone to say that he simply had a dream while he was in an induced coma. Possibly even a hallucination because of the pain medicine he was on. I'm sure there are people who believe that there is no way he went to Heaven and came back again. And that is perfectly okay. It isn't my job to force people to believe or to convince them that it is true. It is my task to simply be the voice of our story and share it with others.

I remember telling everyone shortly after the accident that I believed that Jackson had had an experience in Heaven. How did I know? Simple. You could feel it every time you walked into his room in the NICU. The minute you were in Jackson's presence, a feeling of peace and calm would wash over you. There were times I would just sit in his room to find the quiet and stillness that my soul longed for.

It would be another nine months before he would mention his trip to Heaven again. Thankfully, I had the presence of mind to record that conversation as well as future conversations. I wanted to be able to show anyone who ever doubted Jackson's experience that this was coming from him and him alone. I didn't put ideas in his head or lead him to answers. He spoke, and I listened. The only thing I ever allowed myself to do was clarify things that he said. This way no one could ever accuse me of "putting words in his mouth" or giving him ideas.

The next conversation was during the week of the one-year anniversary of the accident. We were on our way home from school, and, as we always did, we were chitchatting about his day at school and everything he had learned. I cannot remember what triggered the conversation, but he decided to talk about his trip to Heaven. He explained to me that the process of dying was instantaneous. You simply close your eyes and wake up in Heaven. The example he gave was that if you get shot and die, you're in Heaven before your body ever reaches the ground. He shared with me that Jesus gave him the power to walk on the clouds because he didn't have wings like everyone else did. You only receive your wings when you're dead, and he wasn't dead yet. He told me about the gates made of gold. (I later showed him pictures of Heaven's gates, and he picked out the one made of pearls. I assume he didn't know that pearls would shine too.) He told me that everyone there was middle aged and that they were the same color in Heaven that they had been on earth. There was no pain, no fear, or sadness in Heaven. He explained that since his name wasn't written in the Book of Life, he had to come back to earth, and he was okay with that because he didn't want to leave his family yet. He excitedly told me, "The last time I remember walking is walking in Heaven with Jesus." Yes, that brought on the waterworks. How awesome is it that the last time he remembers walking, it was beside Jesus?!?!

Jackson knew before waking up in the NICU that he would be paralyzed because Jesus showed him a wheelchair and told him that he would be okay. He explained that before you could even think of something in Heaven, it was instantly there.

He would later share with me that during the wreck, everything went black. When he opened his eyes, he saw stairs and a light. At the top of the stairs, Jesus was waiting for him. As he got closer to Jesus, a "good feeling" started washing over his body. On his trip home, an angel came to bring him back to earth, and everything once again went black. When he opened his eyes, he was on a stretcher looking up into a paramedic's eyes. The paramedics who worked the scene of the accident later confirmed that it was entirely possible that Jackson could have died on the scene, as his vitals were all over the place while they desperately tried to stabilize him.

Recently, on our trip home there was a beautiful ray of sunshine coming through the clouds. It was simply stunning. Jackson looked at it and told me that it was similar to the light he saw while going in to Heaven. I had been thinking a lot of my Nannie, who died only a few months before the accident. I simply adored my grandmother and had never had the proper time to process her death when the accident happened. Since I was her only caregiver, her death was even more difficult for me to go through. I have mentioned before that I had an extremely difficult childhood. My Nannie was the ray of sunlight leading me on. She encouraged me. She taught me about life's lessons. She loved with her whole heart, and as far as I know, she never told a single lie in her entire life. She was who I wanted to be when I grew up! So before I could even think about what I was saying, I asked Jackson if he had seen my Nannie during his trip to Heaven.

He told me, "No, I didn't get to see her because she was on the other side of Heaven's gates, toward the back where the judging angel was." He mentioned that he got to see God while in Heaven.

So I asked, "What did He look like?"

He told me that he could see Him but not really, because His light hurt his eyes, because God was so bright. Again, these are not things he could have ever known that the Bible confirmed to be true.

The things he has shared with me are biblical. You could say he got the idea of clouds and Jesus from church or pictures he had possibly seen. However, he had attended church only a couple of times prior to the accident, as we had only recently started attending church together as a family. I assure you, our church didn't talk about the

Book of Life or what age people would be in Heaven. He simply knows too much that is verified by the Word for it to be a coincidence, a dream, or a hallucination.

Occasionally, something will spark Jackson's memory, and he will casually mention something that he remembers about Heaven. We know that there is more to his experience than he has already shared, but it is up to him to decide when he is ready to talk about it. It is his story to share. We believe that Jackson has a purpose on this earth, and he will accomplish that purpose, either standing or sitting in a wheelchair. Jackson's experience in Heaven and what he decides to share about it is between God and Jackson.

To this day, people ask me how Jackson handles being paralyzed. They are amazed when I tell them that he is the happiest kid I have ever known. His smile brightens up any room. His laughter is like a balm to your soul. I believe with everything that is in me it is because he was in the presence of Jesus and he brought some of Heaven back with him.

—∞—

I couldn't see God's face because it was too bright. He was there, though.

Jackson

—∞—

I share Jackson's story because if you have ever doubted that there is a God or that Heaven exists, you don't have to anymore. Heaven is real, and, most importantly, God is real. If you have lost someone you love, one day you *will* see that person again. You are never alone. God is ready to engulf you with His grace and mercy. He wants to wrap you up in His loving embrace. All you have to do is let Him in.

CHAPTER 10

—⚊⚊ ⟊ ⚊⚊—

God has said, "I will never fail you.
I will never abandon you."

HEBREWS *13:5 NLT*

October 19, 2015 (Facebook post)

IT IS HARD to admit you are not Superwoman with unlimited amounts of energy and time, but today I will come forth and say I am no Superwoman. I am trying to do all I can here in Atlanta to get our home ready for Jackson on limited sleep and resources. I am overwhelmed and sleep deprived so will be a little selfish by asking for prayers for myself.

October 20, 2015 (Facebook post)

I finally got some sleep! God listens to our prayers so thank you to everyone who prayed! Looking forward to seeing what this day has in store for Jackson and me. Please continue to pray that P.J. has the support he needs as we continue to get our home ready for Jackson. Only nine more days until our family is together again! #JacksonStrong

October 21, 2015 (Facebook post)

Today was the first time since the accident that Jackson cried. He has to use a loaner wheelchair to leave the hospital in while we work with insurance and the manufacturer for his, and he doesn't feel comfortable in it. Until now, he *hasn't complained once about his circumstances or what anyone asks him to do. I asked the staff to give him the hospital wheelchair back. Such a small thing to be upset about, but to him it was a huge deal. Please pray that they get him a new one here before we leave or make adjustments to this one that he feels comfortable with.*

It was difficult for me to sleep during this time. I was becoming more and more exhausted as every day went by. There comes a point when the adrenaline from a traumatic event starts to wear off and you begin to transition into your "new" life. Yes, I was physically exhausted, but the emotional exhaustion was really creeping up on me. There were so many house repairs and things to do in order to bring Jackson home. So much to learn at Scottish Rite about how to care for Jackson once we were able to return home. We learned very quickly that any type of medical equipment Jackson needed would ultimately require lots of hours on the phone with the insurance company and some begging and pleading thrown in for good measure. We were beginning to learn just how expensive it would be for us and later in life for Jackson.

October 22, 2015 (Facebook post)
Today is a BIG day! We are going on a field trip to the museum! This will be the first time Jackson has left the hospital since his accident (other than the ambulance transport to Atlanta). Until now, he has only been in a hospital environment surrounded by other kids in wheelchairs, so this will be a new experience for him. Also, the first time in a vehicle after such a tragic accident is always difficult. So please take a moment prayer warriors to pray that Jackson has a GREAT day, free from fear and stress!

C.C. and Jackson at the Fernbank Museum

October 23, 2015 (Facebook post)

Jackson had a blast on his first outing since the accident! He was nervous about wrecking at first, but decided Jesus saved him the first time so it would be okay. Seriously, how lucky are we to have such an awesome kid!?!

There were moments when he and I realized just how much our lives have changed. You don't think about things being handicap accessible until you need them to be. Life isn't as simple as just running up a flight of stairs anymore. There are things that he wants to do but can't. He wanted to do something as simple as climb up into a tree house. Jackson, being the kid he is, told me to just put him on the floor and he would scoot up it somehow. I pray that he continues to push me and everyone around him when he is told that he can't do something!

Please continue to pray for our family. The hardest part of our journey will begin when we get home and learn to adjust to our "new" normal.

The field trip to the Fernbank Museum was very important for a couple of reasons. First, Jackson was finally allowed to "break out of this joint," as he liked to say. He literally hadn't left the hospital since the day of the wreck. He had been transported to Scottish Rite in an ambulance when he was still a very sick little boy, so it didn't really count as "getting to leave." This would be the first time he would get to leave, and we were both very excited about it. He would finally get to see the outside of a hospital.

When it was time to go, he rolled himself to the front of the building to get loaded on the bus. The excitement on his face warmed my heart. Finally, all the children were loaded and headed for the museum in Atlanta. I quickly learned why this field trip was a part of the curriculum at Scottish Rite. It was the first glimpse at seeing what our "new" life would soon be like on a day to day basis. Traveling with Jackson in a wheelchair would definitely be different from what we were used to and would require more thought for us to be prepared for every possibility. I had to keep a schedule of every time he needed to be catheterized (this was now the only way he could urinate, as he did not have control of his bodily functions due to the spinal cord injury). I needed to make sure he "weight shifted" every thirty minutes (to prevent pressure sores on his bottom). I would now have to carry a diaper bag for medical supplies such as catheters, diapers, wipes, and extra clothing since he was unable to be on a bowel program. Most people who suddenly became paralyzed can typically get on a bowel program, meaning they can have bowel movements only on digital stimulation, helping to avoid accidents in public. Jackson was the exception because he lost over half of his bowels during his many surgeries due to the infection caused from his colon rupturing during the accident. I worried about how this would affect him when he returned to school, but of course Jackson took it all in stride.

Even opening a door while trying to push his wheelchair was a new experience. I learned quickly to appreciate the kindness of others who simply opened the door for us when entering a building. I knew that people would stare at him. It was simply human nature for people to wonder why he was in a wheelchair. This didn't concern me whatsoever, because I knew that it was something that Jackson would have to learn to deal with at some point. I also discovered that day that stairs would never be an option for our family. I have always had such a huge fear of elevators, afraid of being trapped inside one. I quickly came to terms that this was a fear I would have to overcome.

I also knew there would be things Jackson wouldn't be able to do. It was difficult for me because from the very first moment, I learned to change the way I talked to him. Our conversations were based on what he could do, trying to find ways that he could do things, despite his being in a wheelchair. At the museum, there was a tree house that kids were able crawl through and climb up to the top. For the first time, there was something that he simply would not be able to do. Yes, he could crawl through, but that risked the chance of rug burns (he can't feel pain, so this was likely). There was simply no way he would be able to crawl up the tree. He didn't have the upper body strength. At this point, he could sit up for only a few seconds at a time without assistance.

I dreaded saying no to him, because I didn't want him to dwell on the one thing he couldn't do. I wanted him to think about all of the other things he could do. I knew Jackson would be okay when he went through a list of options as to how he could get to the top of the tree house, including trying to get me to lift him up there, which wasn't happening.

This would be the first time we would encounter something he couldn't do, but definitely not the last. It continues to be a daily struggle. We know he simply can't do everything that he wants, yet it is our job to continuously teach him how to think about ways that he can. As long as he has the spirit of an overcomer, Jackson will succeed. Sometimes we hear the word "no." There are things we can't do. Hear me out before you gasp in horror. I will never be a famous singer. There are not enough voice lessons on the planet to help me become a singer, much less a famous one. We are taught we can do anything, as long as we put our mind and effort into it. We should always strive to overcome the odds. The truth is, there are things in life that we will not be able to do. But that doesn't mean we should just throw our hands up in the air and give up. We should continue forward, learning the things that we can do. I can't sing, but if I truly love singing, I could learn about the recording industry and go into the field that way. The point is, find a way to be involved in what you love. Our paths do not always take a direct route. Sometimes we experience a few detours along the way.

October 23, 2015 (Facebook post)
(Pam Smith—Family Friend)
We are going to volunteer to help the family fort the kids that had the car wreck. Several of my ladies that work with me has already been there several days. So proud of Susie Melton, Kathy Tramel, & Tisha Vandergriff ! I'm also going today to try to help finish the painting. There have been so many to help this family. It's so great! C.C.. Hasty Andrews & her family still have a long road ahead. But at least this will help. So proud to be able to help this family. I haven't gotten to help much, but every little thing will help! My sister, Susie Melton got several of the girls involved!!!

This woman is one of the greatest women I have ever had the privilege to meet. When everyone else bailed, she stepped in to help. Her team spent over a week at our home, without pay, painting and helping to get our home ready for Jackson. Have you ever met someone who has the purest of hearts you have ever known, and that person spent his or her life making sacrifices to simply help others? That is Pam Smith and everyone who works for her.

October 24, 2015 (Facebook post)
In less than a week we will all be home together again!

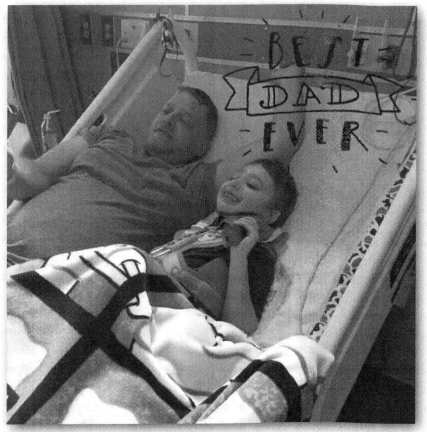

P.J. and Jackson Playing the Wii at Scottish Rite

October 24, 2015 (Facebook post)
My husband and I have switched positions again and I am now home trying to hurry to get the construction finished, construction cleanup done and the house put back together again before Wednesday. It was hard leaving Jackson's smiling face but I am so thankful that he loves to FaceTime me.

Please pray that everything falls into place and that we get the help that we need to get it done in time. It was a huge undertaking in such a short time frame but it will totally be worth the stress, sleepless nights and expense when Jackson comes home to a house that he can feel free in!

When I got home, I thought about heading back to Atlanta to kill my husband. Our home was a complete and utter disaster. Not just from the construction, but from everything being moved from room to room. There were mountains of furniture and clutter. Each room had a huge pile in the center of it that I had to untangle and put back together. I had expected to clean up sawdust. I had not expected to completely move back into our home again while simultaneously cleaning it. Overwhelmed doesn't begin to describe how I felt. To make matters worse, my husband had persuaded the doctors to let them come home a week early. So instead of having a week to get it done, I had only a couple of days.

October 27, 2015 (Facebook post)
A HUGE thank you to Josh Carney for spending his entire day taking me to Atlanta and driving P.J.'s truck home so that we can leave together as a family!!!

A year before our boys' accident, my good friend Josh Carney was also involved in an automobile accident with his son, Mason. I was on Facebook and saw a friend's post saying that they had both been critically injured and LifeFlighted to Vanderbilt Hospital. My heart broke for him, and I felt so helpless. What could I do to help? I knew rushing to the hospital wasn't the answer. Josh would have a ton of family and friends there to support him. All I could do was spread the word and ask for prayers They would ultimately spend weeks at Vanderbilt Children's Hospital and then be transferred to Scottish

Rite in Atlanta for Mason to undergo intense physical therapy. During that time, I was able to witness his family's journey through social media and television interviews. I remembered how thankful I was to be kept up to date on his and his son's progress. I watched as they were able to overcome the odds as Mason continued to do more than the doctors could ever hope for. I felt as if I were a part of their journey.

So when I started to receive calls from local media networks for interviews, I called Josh. I was thankful to have someone who had walked in my shoes. He knew what I felt, the questions that I needed to have answers to. He was able to guide me through the process and what to expect. He was also the first person I thought of when I found out Jackson would be released from Scottish Rite early, because I knew he would understand our need to keep Jackson's coming home private.

—m—

It certainly hit home for me. I remember the rush of emotions I experienced when I first found out about the accident. It brought back familiar feelings of panic and despair. But one thing I knew for certain was that God can replace those feelings of helplessness with feelings of hope, as He did with my family. Like so many others, I called upon the Lord in prayer, asking for mercy on the Andrews family. God was in control of their journey of healing, and we used this time to help encourage others as well. I am one of countless blessed by the stories surrounding this event on a daily basis. It has been made apparent to me that anything is possible when you have complete trust in

God. Having seen the difficult struggles and great triumphs of the Andrews family, I stand here both thankful and amazed.

Josh Carney, family friend

—⚓—

It was important for our family to be home together without everyone showing up at one time to see Jackson. I knew how much everyone missed him, but I didn't want Jackson to be overwhelmed. It was important that we would be able to spend time together as a family first. This was the first time he would be home in months, and it would be a transition for him and for the other brothers. They hadn't been able to see their brother since he had left for Scottish Rite. Josh would understand this need. He immediately stepped up to the task and offered to take off work to drive me all the way to Atlanta just to turn around and come back home on the same day.

October 28, 2015 (Facebook post)
Urgent prayer request: Alex has been rushed to the hospital. Please pray!

Unbeknownst to everyone when I posted this on Facebook, we were on our way home with Jackson. We had only been driving for about an hour when Jackson suddenly went into a mild autonomic dysreflexia (AD) attack. AD is a life-threatening emergency that affects patients with T6 and higher spinal cord injuries. Jackson's injury is a T1, meaning we would have to constantly be on guard and watchful. It causes high blood pressure, headaches, flushed face, spots on his body, and severe sweating, just to name a few symptoms. It can cause the patient to have a stroke, which can lead to death. Something as simple as a pebble being in his shoe that is irritating him without his knowledge can cause AD.

I can't explain to you how scared my husband and I were. Here we were, for the first time ever, leaving with Jackson, and the unthinkable was happening. We contemplated finding the nearest hospital to rush him to, or turning around and heading straight back to Scottish Rite. As we were stripping him down in the back seat trying to find the source of his discomfort, I received a phone call that Alex needed to be rushed to the hospital. We were at some random convenience store somewhere on the side of the interstate with one son who was having his first medical crisis outside of the hospital while in our care, and another son was over three hours away being rushed to the hospital. I would like to say that this was completely surprising and took us off guard. Unfortunately, this was our new normal. Nothing would ever be easy or simple anymore. Once again, I felt helpless. I did the only thing I could do: ask for prayers.

October 28, 2015 (Facebook post)
Update on Alex: he is at home now and resting. There are multiple diagnoses at the moment but I do not want to share until I feel comfortable knowing for certain what is going on. Please continue to pray for him as he is in a lot of pain and very sick. I am sometimes amazed at how the devil comes to our joy. And this is exactly that. What should be a time of celebration as our family is reunited the devil tries to take it away. But the good news is God is the truth and the devil is a liar. Our family has been through so much, and because of it so many people's lives have been touched. Obviously, the devil wants us to be afraid and he wants me to shut up. However, I ain't ever been one to cower down and I am not going to start now. So, here's the

truth...God's word is true today and always. He is the ultimate healer. He has brought my family this far and He is always victorious. On this I stand. #JacksonStrong

October 29, 2015 (Facebook post)

Our family tends to think of our lives in two stages. Before the accident and after the accident. It is as if there was a line drawn in time for our family. From the outside looking in, you would think that everything after would be tragic and heartbreaking. It isn't. Our family has been changed beyond imagination. We are stronger. We are closer. Our faith has grown beyond measure. We're able to witness God in all of His wonder and glory. And we get to experience all of these "new" firsts together. Our boys are alive. I pray that our lives never get so busy and mundane again that we forget to appreciate what God has allowed us to have. As Jackson said yesterday looking at the car that changed his life forever, "It was just an accident but we are all okay now." Yes, Jackson, we most definitely are!

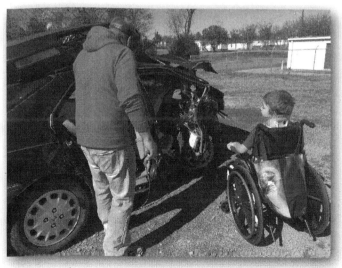

Jackson Seeing the Car for the First Time

CHAPTER 11

Let the morning bring me word of your unfailing love, for I have put my trust in you. Show me the way I should go, for to you I entrust my life.

PSALM *143:8 NIV*

November 1, 2015 (Facebook post)
(Pam Smith—Family Friend)
THIS LITTLE GUY is stronger than most grown-ups. We had a really great time at the benefit today! Thank you so much C.C. Hasty Andrews for taking a picture of me and Jackson together. His smile means more to me than anything. I'm so thankful we all could be a part of his life. He is a very special young man. You are a special person also, C.C. He's lucky to have you for his mom!

As we were busy preparing to bring Jackson home, several of our family and friends were busy preparing to hold a benefit for Jackson to help raise money for an FES bike (Functional Electrical Stimulation). The FES bike would help Jackson keep his legs strong and healthy. I had been to benefits before for other people, but I had never thought that my family would be the recipient of one. I didn't know what to expect, but I knew that for the first time since the accident, I would need to speak about our story with people I had never personally met. Up until this point, we had lived in hospitals. Our only focus had been to take care of our kids. I was such a prideful person before the accident, and I was just learning how to accept things from others. I was normally a very reserved person, and I didn't talk about things going on in my life. Now I would be expected to. Surprisingly, I ended up discovering that I loved to talk to people about our story and how much God had done for our family. I finally felt that I was doing exactly what God was calling me to do. This was exactly where God wanted me to be. Every moment had led me to this one. The benefit was absolutely beautiful and we all had such a fun time meeting some of the people who had been praying and supporting our family.

I could write paragraph after paragraph naming the people who helped our family along the way. Early on, I felt it was a requirement or an obligation to publicly announce what people had done to help our family. Although it is contradictory, it almost felt like a burden. How would I ever repay everyone for what they had done? I would never be able to do enough things in my lifetime to pay back what had been done for our family. Shortly after the benefit, I called Josh Carney, my friend who had been in an accident with his son, to talk about how I felt. I shared with him my feelings of inadequacy. He had also felt that way, and to this day still does to a certain extent. I learned that it was normal to feel this way, and because I did, it also made me human. What kind of person would I be if I expected people to go out of their way for my family? A grateful heart is a thankful heart, and I was thankful for each and every person who freely gave of his or her time and resources.

November 2, 2015 (Facebook post)
(P.J.)

I am thankful that my boys that are still with us today through this life changing event. Here is a picture of C.C. reading Jack a bedtime story and a picture of Josh rocking out on the drums tonight at the benefit. Love you guys!

November 2, 2015 (Facebook post)

While at Vanderbilt yesterday, I was able to take a few moments to sit on the bench that was my "thinking" spot during our time there. I noticed how much had changed: the color of the leaves turning during Fall, the cooler temperatures, people dressed in warmer clothes. But most importantly, I realized just how much I had changed. My faith grew stronger on that bench as I spent time there with God. My heart healed a little more every day as the bodies of my children healed. As I sat there, I praised God for His blessings. Alex started back to school part-time. Jackson was able to have the neck brace removed, which will provide him more mobility and allow him to progress faster with physical therapy. We received a check in the mail from a perfect stranger that we desperately needed. And all of that was just yesterday! As I sat on my "thinking" bench, I knew that God didn't bring us here to leave us here. I also know that God didn't put Jackson in that wheelchair to leave him there either! We still have challenges ahead, but God has and will carry us forward with His grace and mercy.

November 3, 2015 (Facebook post)

The schools have been absolutely fabulous with our boys since the accident. Ms. Neeley and all of the staff at Community Elementary and Middle School have done everything they can to transition and accommodate them back into school. Cascade High School has Alex still on track to graduate this year. In fact, Scottish Rite told us they had never dealt with a more professional or helpful school district! You don't hear enough good about the school system and I just wanted to share how thankful we are for all they have done!

—⁂—

The only time I have been able to walk after becoming paralyzed was when I walked with Jesus.

Jackson

—⁂—

November 5, 2015 (Facebook post)
Today, while I was carrying Jackson from one mattress to another at Kincaid's Furniture Store, he told me that my arms were comfy. I said, "More comfy than that chair you want?" He said, "Yes, more comfy than anything else in the entire world." I am not certain that anything else said to me by anyone in this entire world would have made me any happier. To know that he feels safe and comfortable in my arms is the highest form of praise I could ever be given! I also want to give a huge thank you to Kincaid's for offering us 50% off the items Jackson needs!

Even on good days, being a stepparent is difficult. When my husband and I married, I knew that we would ultimately receive full custody of his three boys. I accepted that his children were a part of him and therefore a part of our marriage. My husband and I have had an untold number of disagreements, to put it nicely, about how to raise our children, especially when it involves one of our biological children. There are a multitude of factors that are involved in raising children in a blended family, and sometimes we simply do not agree. There are also a lot of fears. Am I making the right decisions? Have I treated them equally and fairly? Will they ever understand why I made the decisions that I made? These are all pretty normal when parenting, whether it be your child or a stepchild. There just seems to be a little more pressure involved when parenting stepchildren. When our boys make comments like the one above, I know that they are sincere. It lets me know that I am indeed being a good stepparent.

November 10, 2015 (Facebook post)

Today as I was showing a visitor pictures of Jackson from our trip to the beach and Disney World right before the accident, my heart ached from seeing him be able to run and play. As I was settling in to study in my brand-new Bible tonight, the very first page I turned to and verse I read was Acts 14:8. "In Lystra they met a man who had been crippled since birth; his feet were completely useless. He listened to Paul speak, and Paul could see in this man's face that he had faith to be healed. Paul said, 'Stand up on your own two feet, man!' The man jumped up and walked!" Some could say it was a coincidence, but luckily, I don't believe in coincidences. I believe in a God that reminded me when I needed it most He has the final say if and when Jackson will walk again. I believe he will not only walk, but he will RUN!!! #JacksonStrong

Sometimes God talks to us through a knowing inside our heart, sometimes it's through other people, and sometimes it's through scripture. I knew when I read this scripture that it was from God. By this point we had accepted that Jackson would never walk again. That is not something one easily comes to terms with. It took a long time to finally accept it. And although we know that the likelihood of Jackson walking again is very slim, we also believe that God is capable of anything. God told me on the side of that road on that August day that He had a plan and a purpose for this, and that included Jackson's paralysis. But I don't believe that He brought us here to leave us here. Jackson has a plan and purpose for his life, and he will accomplish it, standing or sitting.

CHAPTER 12

———— ·~· ————

Cast all your anxiety on him because he cares for you.

1 PETER 5:7 NIV

YOU WOULD THINK that our family had experienced enough tragedy to last a lifetime. We had fought together and stayed together. We were finally home, together as a family. Now we would finally learn to live this new life together that God had given us.

But over the course of the next few months, my life would be flipped and turned upside down in every way imaginable. Our story was just beginning.

November 12, 2015 (Facebook post)
Alex has been rushed back to the hospital and is in a lot of pain. Please pray that we finally find answers and that his pain is alleviated.

November 13, 2015 (Facebook post)
Alex is being admitted into the hospital with Acute Pancreatitis. Not what we were hoping for but at least now we have a definite answer and can start treatment. We don't know the exact cause yet but it is possibly from the trauma to his stomach during the accident. Please pray for a speedy recovery and for us parents who are now once again separated. Tonight makes only the second

time I have cried in front of doctors, the first being the day we found out that Jackson was paralyzed. It was just one day too many of watching one of my kids cry in pain and being helpless to make it go away. I try to be this physically and emotionally strong woman for my family, but tonight I am just tired and exhausted.

November 13, 2015 (Facebook post)
No matter how much bigger he is than me, he will always be my baby. It's killing me to watch him scream and cry from the pain. He hasn't gotten a break from it since yesterday around noon. No amount of pain medication is even touching it. Please pray that the pain eases up soon.

I knew the first time that Alex was rushed to the hospital while we were bringing Jackson home from Scottish Rite that the diagnosis our local hospital gave him was not correct. As a mother, I intuitively knew that there was something else going on. Yet our local emergency room and his primary care physician could not figure out what it was. I had them check for pancreatitis during his very first visit to the emergency room, but of course they missed it.

I tried to rush Alex back to Vanderbilt, which is a little over an hour away from our home, but he simply couldn't make it. Somehow, I knew that he wouldn't survive the drive, and I was right. So I took him to a hospital in Murfreesboro, Tennessee, which is between our home and Nashville. They made us wait for several hours while Alex screamed and cried in pain. This kid who had overcome the odds, never complained, and had even just started to walk again was begging for help. He should have been considered a high priority case since I told them he was having a pancreatic attack, because I had suspected pancreatitis all along. Yet we waited and waited. Out of desperation,

I loaded him back into the car to try to make it to Vanderbilt. I had to pull over on the side of the road less than a mile from the hospital and call an ambulance. I knew that the paramedics would make Alex a priority case and take him back immediately, and they did. This was my first indication that things were not going to go well at this hospital.

After the first twenty-four hours after the accident, we knew what was wrong with each child. And although Jackson would spend over a month fighting for his life due to infection, we knew what was wrong with him and were prepared for it. This time, we had no idea what was wrong with Alex or how to help him.

I thought that seeing him in pain with his leg in traction was horrible. I didn't think it could get any worse than seeing him in pain after the acute compartment syndrome. I was wrong. The pain he was in was relentless, and no amount of pain medication could take it away. Hour after hour, day after day, it never let up. I would sit in my vehicle in the parking lot just to cry so that Alex wouldn't see me. I pleaded with God to take it away. I would have gladly taken it from him if I could. I didn't know that the human body could experience that level of pain for that long. With pancreatitis, pain management is key. If you cannot control the pain, then the more chances the patient will not survive.

November 14, 2015 (Facebook post)
Alex is finally sleeping in spurts, which means I too was able to catch a few hours of sleep. The pain is still significant but showing signs of decreasing. He is still very nauseous as well. Also, I found out this morning that someone I loved like a father passed away yesterday. Please continue to keep our family in your prayers. Thank you! #JacksonStrong

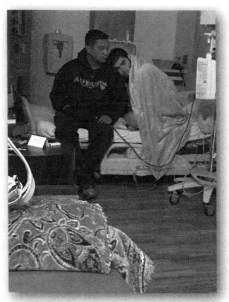

Alex and His Father Carlos at Saint Thomas Rutherford Hospital

And then, when I didn't think it could get worse, it did. Two days after Alex was admitted into the hospital, I accidentally discovered that my husband had been texting my best friend's twenty-year-old daughter. At first, I thought it was perhaps something to do with a vehicle he was possibly working on as he owned an auto repair shop, but conversations about vehicle repair don't happen at two o'clock in the morning. I couldn't believe it. I had to be wrong. I had known her since she was barely eight years old. She ran up to me and hugged me every time I saw her. This was like being stuck in a nightmare.

I was spending day after day with my son in the hospital, who was possibly dying. Yet my husband, who couldn't find the time to come visit us in the hospital, was busy flirting with a twenty-year-old girl. I couldn't fathom it. He was supposed to be my support system. The one I could always count on and lean on when the weight of the world felt too heavy to carry. But I realized that from the first moment after the accident, I had really always been alone. He was never emotionally present for me as I was for him. I decided not to tell him that I knew, because matters such as adultery were simply on the bottom of the list of priorities. The life of my son came first.

Men most always cheat because they are seeking emotional fulfillment. Our marriage had been in trouble for the past year. The sudden change in our lives from receiving full custody of his boys, starting new businesses, and all the financial difficulties that arose from that had simply been too much. Instead of pulling together, we pulled further apart from each other.

We were in marriage counseling working on our issues when the accident happened. I thought we had gotten past all of that and were moving forward as a family. I was incredibly mistaken. He simply couldn't handle the stress of the accident, but most importantly, he couldn't handle being alone. Although our month-long separations had not been my fault, he had also felt alone. He needed companionship and attention when I was not in a position to give it. I was in the hospital once again with my son and could in no way offer the emotional support he needed. Yes, he should have supported me as I supported him, but women tend to handle emotional crises much better than men—which is ironic, considering women are always the ones being accused of being too emotional in relationships.

So I kept my silence and carried on as if none of it were happening. It was really the only choice I had.

—⁂—

We were exhausted and simply not walking in love. We grew more distant from each other as every day passed. We were both caught up in our own fears instead of trying to help each other. Because we were both in separate hospitals, the divide between us grew greater and greater. Without God, there was no way our marriage would have survived.

P.J., the boys' dad

—⁂—

November 15, 2015 (Facebook post)
Urgent Prayer Request: Alex has an infection in his pancreas as well as pancreatitis. We are waiting on cultures to see if the infection has traveled to his blood. CT scans show that his pancreas is getting worse instead of better so we are being transferred to a surgeon. Vanderbilt is full but has the best GI specialist in middle Tennessee. Alex has been put on the waiting list. Please pray that the surgeon is able to take his case and that a bed opens up immediately. We need all of our prayer warriors now!

November 15, 2015 (Facebook post)
There are no beds available at Vanderbilt, so the specialist is consulting the doctor here. As of this evening, he has started to get a fever that we cannot break. He is getting sicker by the hour. Please pray that the doctors

are making good decisions and that we get transferred to a facility that is capable of the care that he needs. Although my heart is aching and my mind is screaming in fear, I know that God has a purpose for this. I believe that His word is the same yesterday, today and forever...I also know that ALL things are given to those that believe and have faith. Where two or more come together...So, stand with me in faith that Alex will receive his miraculous healing.

November 16, 2015 (Facebook post)

Update: We had a pretty rough night as the pain pump wasn't on the right setting and the nurses just wouldn't listen to us. After demanding to see the doctor this morning, it has been corrected and he is finally resting now. His labs are showing improvement, which means we are headed in a good direction. He will have another contrast dye CT scan tomorrow to see if any of the swelling has abated in his pancreas. His white blood count is showing improvement and the preliminary culture came back negative, although we won't know for certain for another two to five days. He has pneumonia and a UTI as well, but is on the right antibiotics to treat those. We have denied permission to do a PIC line, and are trying to avoid it all costs while here at Saint Thomas. This update is long I know, but I wanted our prayer warriors to know that your prayers are making a difference and we desperately need them to keep coming!

November 17, 2015 (Facebook post)

(Kyla Arroyo—Alex's Stepmom)
Just wanted to give a heartfelt thank you to everyone who has offered their prayers, good thoughts and kind, reassuring words regarding Alex. He is tough and is by nature a fighter so I look forward to the day we can reflect back on these trying times with pride and joy at the never-ending determination and

perseverance that has been and continues to what be the driving force of Alex's recovery. We love and appreciate all of you.

November 17, 2015 (Facebook post)

After a couple of days of no sleep, I am probably not in the best frame of mind to go head to head with Saint Thomas Rutherford Hospital, but that's exactly what I intend to do today. I have been so very patient with the nursing staff, although I am sure they think differently. What they don't realize is I have lived in a hospital for over three months now. I know what compassionate nursing care should be. I shouldn't have to tell them how to do their job. I am not going to be friendly when my son has blood continuously running into his IV, or he is screaming and gagging from pain because you're an hour late on medication. I don't really care if you're understaffed, that is the administrations responsibility, not mine. I usually never complain, because I know the typical outcome is retaliation toward the patient. In this instance, I honestly don't think the level of care he receives could get any worse. Please pray for me today. I need patience in abundance. For God to give me wisdom when communicating my concerns and for Him to guard my tongue, because I am seriously furious.

November 17, 2015 (Facebook post)

Update: Someone today messaged me and told me it was okay to have messy days. Today was one of them. I do not like to feel as angry and helpless as I did today while trying to get my son the help he needed. I am sure the doctor probably thought I was a lunatic. I know the nurse, who incorrectly told my son he needed to wait five more hours for more pain meds and reinforced it by writing it on his room board, believes beyond a shadow of a doubt that I am. To be honest, I don't care and I'm not sorry. For the first time in six days, Alex has slept. Every single bit of it was worth just that alone. Although we are not *out of the woods yet and he may have to possibly have emergency surgery soon, I feel like I can breathe a little. Please continue to pray for Alex. Pray for the doctors and nurses who treat him (his nurse tonight held his hand and prayed with him). Pray for healing. Pray for answers. P. S. I was able to see Jackson for a few minutes today and he finally got his new loaner wheels! I have attached pictures for all of those who miss seeing him too! #JacksonStrong*

I had felt helpless before. I knew fear. But until this moment, I hadn't really experienced the power of fear in its full glory. I went into the meeting with the administration fully prepared to gain the outcome I was seeking. I wanted my son to be transferred to Vanderbilt or another facility in Nashville immediately. At this point, any hospital other than Saint Thomas Rutherford would have been just fine by me. His pain level was simply too high for me to try to attempt to transfer him myself or we would have already left. If I should call an ambulance to transfer him, insurance would not pay for any of his hospital stay, and the other facility could refuse him. I could no longer tolerate rude nurses and being tossed from one doctor to another, who all had varying opinions. I knew that if we did nothing, he would die. It was really that simple.

During my meeting with the administration, I quickly learned that I had no say-so in the medical decisions for my son. You would think that as a patient who is literally paying for their services, we could choose to be transferred to another hospital. Yet they wouldn't release him. Refused, in fact. I didn't even know that was a possibility. I believed it was because by doing so they would be admitting fault and wrongdoing. I didn't care. I was just trying to save my son's life. They had missed several things that should have been obvious, including a urinary tract infection and c-diff, which he contracted during his stay at their facility. We later learned that most of the patients on the seventh floor had c-diff. Considering that nurses and doctors who knew how contagious c-diff was continued to come into Alex's room without gloves and protective gear, I could clearly see why. C-diff is a bacterial infection in the colon that causes severe abdominal cramps and diarrhea. Imagine the stomach flu times ten. Now imagine having c-diff on top of pancreatitis, which many doctors have told us is the most severe pain a person can endure. One doctor even told me that their facility was not equipped to handle a case of Alex's level, yet they refused to let us leave.

The hospital administration wanted us to stay so that they could make it up to us and show us that their hospital could provide the care my son needed. See, my post on Facebook reached many people who had been following our story, including people higher up in the pecking order of the hospital's administration. They had received multiple communications regarding my son's case and had been informed that they didn't want the negative publicity I could provide. It sometimes pays to know people, and I was willing to use any resource at my disposal. I left that meeting feeling completely helpless. How could I not be able to choose to send my son to another hospital? We were literally being held hostage. I went outside and cried until I couldn't cry anymore. Then I had to go back to Alex's room, look him in the eyes, and tell him that we had to stay.

Later that very same day, I demanded once again to see the doctor and the administration. Several hours after our meeting, a nurse told Alex to stop being a baby and that his medicine wasn't due for another six hours, so he was going to just have to suck it up. I have never raised my voice to a doctor or nurse, but this time, I did. I made sure that they understood that I would do whatever it took to help my son. When Alex heard the doctor explain why he couldn't be transferred, he looked her square in the face and exclaimed, "You don't care about me. You are going to leave here in your fancy car, eat a fancy dinner while spending time with your family watching *Gray's Anatomy*. I mean nothing to you." I still laugh to this day when I picture that doctor's shocked face at his outburst. Can you imagine being trapped in a hospital by people who you know couldn't care less about you, while you lie there suffering and in pain? That was exactly how Alex felt.

November 18, 2015 (Facebook post)

Update: After meeting with the GI specialist this morning, we have confirmation that Alex's pancreas was injured during the impact from the accident three months ago. They believe he also has a pancreatic bile duct leak that could require surgery and have confirmed definite neurotic or a cyst on his pancreas. This could have a chance to heal itself with proper pain management. Not guaranteed but possible. After my crazy momma show down yesterday, we now have made headway toward controlling the pain. We have decided to wait at least twenty-four hours before deciding if we should have surgery as the pain has just now started to be controlled with medication. Obviously, the risks are there and even more so from this procedure. This is not an option we want to pursue but will if necessary. We need our prayer warriors to stand in agreement with us that the pain continues to lesson and future CT scans reflect improvement soon, as we only have at most forty-eight hours to decide.

November 18, 2015 (Facebook post)

This kid of mine is being so brave and tough. I wish that I could take away his pain and everything he has had to go through during the last three months. I know that when his body and spirit are healed, and I BELIEVE that he will be, he will have one tremendous testimony. At every opportunity, he has asked for prayer, even when his faith has been tested more than most people ever have to face in a lifetime. I have said since the beginning that my boys' faith has been the backbone of mine.

November 19, 2015 (Facebook post)

I need our prayer warriors today. Please pray for healing. Pray for guidance as we make the decision if we should go forward with surgery. My heart says NO, but I need God's wisdom to be certain that it is His will. Share our story on your page, with your friends, coworkers, and perfect strangers. We need God flooded with prayers from HIS people today.

—⁂—

It felt as if we had mountains of trials to overcome. One moment, I would be in one child's room rejoicing for answered prayers and the next moment in another room being given bad news. I felt as if I were on a pendulum swinging back and forth between Heaven and hell. I used to read stories in the Bible about people who would quickly lose their faith, even after God performed miracle after miracle for them and I just couldn't figure out how they forgot God so easily. I didn't have to wonder anymore. I knew exactly how they felt.

C.C., the boys' mom

—⁂—

November 20, 2015 (Facebook post)

Yesterday, I could not wait to post an update that we had turned a corner, but something held me back. Last night, we took another turn for the worse. I am past my breaking point. There is such a lack of communication on the part of the medical staff at Saint Thomas Rutherford. I again need prayers that they either agree to transfer him to another facility or move him into the ICU where he can get the level of care he needs. Please also pray that they have a different GI specialist that can be consulted in. I shouldn't have to ask for prayers that a medical facility do what they need to do to keep my son alive, but I am. I am ready for God to show up and show out!

Alex's father, stepmother, and I went outside to get some fresh air. We confided in one another that we were preparing ourselves for Alex to die. He was that sick. I can still feel the crushing weight of that feeling—believing that I would have to bury my child while knowing that if he could just be transferred to another facility, he might have a chance to live. Yet I was helpless to do anything about it.

November 21, 2015 (Facebook post)

This year has brought some of the most difficult moments of my life. From losing people that I love to almost losing my children. I don't know the plan God has for me and my family, but I know that He has wonderful things in store for us. The devil comes to steal, kill, and destroy. If I am under attack, then the devil sees my boys and me as a threat. My son, who was in so much pain that I thought my heart might literally break from it, started each morning and ended each night asking for prayer. This week when I was consumed with fear, my son reminded me who I needed to call out to. He is the one who gives us peace and hope. When I knew if God didn't intervene my child would die, I went outside and screamed at God. I demanded that He show up and honor His word. It is in those times that God craves from us total surrender. He wants us to call out to Him so that He can do what He promised to do in His word. Today, my son is healing. He now has an infection that we must overcome and we have another long road ahead, but he will heal. The moment things changed for him? That moment when all I could do was cry out to the One who told me to take heart, because He had overcome the world.

November 22, 2015 (Facebook post)

Just wanted to update everyone that Alex is still in the hospital and we are not sure when he will get to come home. Please continue to pray for him and our family!

November 23, 2015 (Facebook post)

As Alex and I prayed last night, God whispered "breakthrough" to me. In that moment, it was hard to conceive. Alex had such a hard day yesterday and was emotionally and physically spent. Last time we had a breakthrough I didn't post it out of fear that it was temporary, and it was. I will no longer allow fear to contradict what God has told me to believe. For the first time in almost two weeks, we slept more than two hours. This morning the nausea has subsided. I saw Alex smile for the first time today. Our breakthrough is here and I am sharing it without fear because I know God has declared it!

Alex begged me to pray with him several times a day. We talked often about his fear of dying, because he was sure that he would never leave the hospital alive. At one point, Alex had a visit from what I believe was an angel that told Alex he would pull through this. I had to remind him of that every time he felt like giving up. My faith had been tested over and over again. But enough was enough. I finally decided that the devil was a liar. I would not allow him to win. I would not cower in fear anymore. Alex would survive this, and God would be the victor. Our prayers began to change. Instead of begging for God's help, we started declaring the victory and praising God for what He *would* do.

November 24, 2015 (Facebook post)

Due to hospital psychosis, the doctor decided Alex would heal better at home, so…we are FINALLY home! Please continue to pray for him as we have a long road of recovery ahead. Thank you to all of our prayer warriors! God heard you and He answered your prayers!

Hospital psychosis, also known as ICU psychosis, can be very dangerous. Some of the causes are sensory deprivation, sleep deprivation, and stress, just to name a few. One of the causes is pain that is not adequately controlled. There are a multitude of symptoms, such as anxiety, hearing voices, hallucinations, agitation, paranoia, and nightmares. I knew he wasn't ready to come home. He still couldn't eat without pain and nausea. But in the back of my mind, all I could think of was escape. This was our way out of Saint Thomas Rutherford! If he was released, we could take him to Vanderbilt, which was exactly what we did the very next day.

—⚏—

The accident changed our family forever. People couldn't possibly understand unless they've been there. To hear the tough young man whom you love as if he were yours wail in agonizing pain while you stand there helpless breaks something deep inside you. Couple that with trying to hold it together so Carlos, C.C., and others have someone to lean on—shew, that's hard! Fearing you could lose your son, fearing you may essentially lose him even if he survives—not to death but to mental anguish as a result of his brothers' injuries…fear of what losing a child would mean for you, your husband, and your other kids, your future…it's torture. That's what I felt from those first uncertain weeks and subsequent hospitalizations. That fear was enough to terrify the most stoic among us.

Kyla Arroyo, Alex's stepmom

—⁓—

November 25, 2015 (Facebook post)
Alex had another pancreatic attack and has been rushed to Vanderbilt by ambulance. Please pray.

November 25, 2015 (Facebook post)
Within fifteen minutes of arriving at Vanderbilt they had Alex pain free. It took Saint Thomas Rutherford six days to accomplish this, and they were really never able to. They are performing an ultrasound now, which again Saint Thomas Rutherford refused to do and told me was unnecessary. God declared he would have his breakthrough and two days ago told Alex He was coming. By tonight we will finally have answers. My heart is finally at peace knowing God has placed us where we need to be.

November 25, 2015 (Facebook post)
Alex's pancreas is still swollen. He is being admitted to Vanderbilt to control his pain and nausea. They will also call in a GI specialist tomorrow. This will be my first Thanksgiving without my Nannie as well as ever being separated

from my family. Although this makes me sad, I am still thankful because now Alex will finally get the help he needs to heal. Whether at home or at Vanderbilt, I will celebrate tomorrow and every day with thanksgiving for all God has done for my family.

I felt such peace having Alex back at Vanderbilt. I knew that he was in the capable hands of the medical staff there, and he would finally be able to heal.

November 26, 2015 (Facebook post)

Alex was brought by ambulance to Vanderbilt yesterday. We have faith that he is now where he needs to be to get better. The doctor informed us this morning that a GI team will be here today as they have discovered he has fluid around his pancreas which may require surgery. Spending Thanksgiving separated as a family is hard, but we are celebrating all that God has done for our family this year and that Alex is finally in the right place to get the help that he needs to heal. Please continue to pray for our family. Thank you and Happy Thanksgiving from our family to yours!

November 27, 2015 (Facebook post)

Who needs sleep when you get to be up to watch a beautiful sunrise over Nashville? Being in a hospital isn't ideal but at least we have one heck of a view! The GI team has decided to wait to do surgery because as they put it, "The number one rule of a surgeon is to never touch the pancreas." They want to see if his body will heal without intrusive measures. The next step will be a feeding tube if he continues to be unable to hold down food or in too much pain from trying. He was able to eat just a little last night and was able to hold it down, so we are making progress! He has also started to get pneumonia. Please continue to pray for healing and for strength for him to get through this.

November 29, 2015 (Facebook post)

Alex was able to eat and hold down food yesterday. His lungs are more clearer and he has barely needed insulin (his pancreas was so severely damaged we were told at Saint Thomas Rutherford he is now a diabetic that will be insulin dependent—of course we believe that God will give him TOTAL healing). He was frustrated this morning because the nurses were waking him up to take his vitals, a good sign that he is definitely getting better. Please continue to pray that he can eat without nausea or pain, the fluid in his lungs clear, and that he can get up and move around some today. We love all of you!

November 30, 2015 (Facebook post)

Alex has been through so much the last four months, yet his faith has only increased. He has shown that he cares more for others than himself by taking care of his brothers, when it mattered most. He has fought for his life, with faith, strength and determination. I am so proud of him and the man he has become. As a child, he was prayed over and told he would do great things for God. I have always believed it and when Alex asked me in the midst of his deepest despair why this was happening to him, I reminded him that, "Unless you have been through the hardest of times and had to rely only on faith alone, how can you help and witnesses to others? God is building you up and strengthening you for His purpose for your life." On August 16th, on the side of that road, God whispered to me that He had a plan a purpose for this. He told Alex to not be afraid, that they would live. He showed himself to Jackson. And, as I watch this child of mine sleep so soundly, I know that God is fulfilling that promise. As I witness Jackson overcome every obstacle in his way, despite his circumstances, my heart is full of joy and pride. I get to be the mom of these wonderful boys who I know beyond a shadow of a doubt are destined to do great things in life.

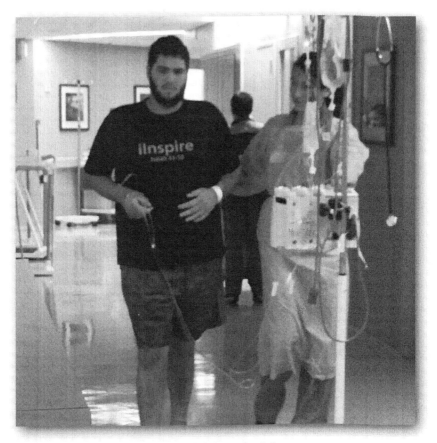

Alex at Vanderbilt Medical Center

CHAPTER 13

*I love the Lord because He hears my
voice and my prayers for mercy.*

PSALM 116:1 NLT

December 1, 2015 (Facebook post)
(Terry, C.C.'s mom)
HOW YOU INSPIRE me. As you know I have had a rough life. I spent a lot
of time feeling sorry for myself. Self-pity. And as you know all too well
bitter for all the things I have been through. Even you as a child needed
me and many times I failed you. Then this tragedy happened and you
brought faith, hope and a pride I never had in myself. You inspire me to
want to be more. I feel so blessed to be your mom and the boys nanny. You
have a strength in you I have never had in myself. In you I see the woman
I wish I could have been. The mother I should have been. My heart swells
with pride watching you with your children and your faith. How so very
blessed I am to be your mother. As much as I feel I let you down, I did one
thing right. I had two wonderful children. When I think of you I think
inspiration. I think God. I think I love you and Chris so much for putting up with me. Thank you for being my daughter and for being such a
wonderful human being. I love you. I love my children and grandchildren.
I AM BLESSED!!!!

December 1, 2015 (Facebook post)
Alex is finally home! He is still in pain but we are praying we can manage
his care at home verses staying in the hospital. Please continue to pray for his
TOTAL healing. Also, I have an unspoken prayer request for myself. Thank
you to all of you who take the time to pray for our family!

The night Alex and I got home, P.J. confronted me. He had guessed
that I somehow knew something was going on. Perhaps it was because I was acting distant or my responses to him were more clipped
than usual. So, instead of my being the one angry and making accusations, he was the one who was angry, blaming me for accusing him
of talking to another girl, which he finally got me to admit I knew
about. He swore up and down he was innocent and that I was the
one who was crazy for believing he would ever do that to me. How
could I ever accuse him of that? I refused to back down because what
he didn't realize was I had seen enough texts to know what he was
doing wasn't innocent. That night, I decided to move into our son's
apartment to help avoid confrontations between us. I hadn't slept in
my bed in weeks. All I wanted to do was curl up in a ball and sleep
for five days straight, but I couldn't. Alex still needed full-time care
and would continue to do so for the next month. I had a son who
needed me and a husband who was simply losing his mind.

We decided to get a divorce and that he would move out as soon as he
found an apartment or a house to rent. I could have forced him, but
I would never do anything to harm our kids or put them in a negative situation. See, I wasn't just losing my husband; I was losing my
children too. I was their stepmother and had been raising them for
almost five years, but I didn't have legal custody of them or rights to

them. It is very difficult to have a stepparent awarded any type of legal rights once there is not a legally binding marriage in place. My heart was breaking. When our family should be coming together, we were instead being ripped apart.

Over the next month, he always somehow found a way to start a screaming match with me. He became this angry and violent person. At one point, he even threw something at me. Who was this person? He most definitely was not the man I had made vows to. That man was long gone. I could hardly speak to the boys without him finding a way to scream at me. It was especially hard on Jackson. We had grown even closer while he was in Atlanta. It hurt me to see him look at me, longing to talk to me but afraid of angering his father if he did. He would gently touch me when I walked by so that his father couldn't see.

P.J. showed no remorse at all for having an affair. When I did finally confront him with undeniable proof, he still refused to even apologize. I just didn't understand it. He was the one who had cheated on me, during one of the most difficult moments in our lives. He let me down, not the other way around. Yet he was the one who was angry. He believed he was the one who had been wronged. When I didn't think it could get any worse, it did.

The only person who kept me sane during all of this was my mother-in-law, Diane. She kept reassuring me that he was having some type of breakdown and that she knew with everything she had in her that he loved me. Deep down I knew this to be true, but a part of me wasn't sure if I could ever handle knowing that he had betrayed me. Even if he wanted me to forgive him, I wasn't sure that I would be able to.

We decided to wait to let everyone know about the divorce until he had moved out of the house and the boys were settled. Although the boys knew something was going on, they didn't know that we had decided to divorce and separate permanently.

December 2, 2015 (Facebook post)
I am looking for a full-time job. Any of my Facebook friends know of a great job with benefits that is hiring fairly quickly?!?! I have a bachelor's degree in Business Management and Human Relations plus seventeen years of administrative experience.

December 4, 2015 (Facebook post)
My life has had more than a normal share of hardship, heartache and trials. At the end of the day, I am thankful because it has made me stronger. I am able to pick myself up and start over, every single time. This new journey my life is taking will be no different. I won't fail, and I don't accept less than what I able to give. Ever.

December 7, 2015 (Facebook post)
Alex had a small pancreatitis attack yesterday but praise God we got through it and didn't have to go back to the hospital. Please continue to pray for him. For heart, body, and mind.

Just before the accident I was offered a position that I knew I would enjoy, but God told me it was not the right timing. I was thankful over the last few months to not have a job that I had to break a commitment to as I would not have been able to fulfill the responsibilities a full-time position would require since the accident. My life has shifted once again and I really need a job to help get through this next journey of my life. I have an interview this morning and would love prayers for favor and for God to open the right doors.

Thank you to everyone who has covered my family with prayers. Just know that they ARE working!

December 8, 2015 (Facebook post)
While messaging Justin yesterday he informs me that the whole time he was actually in the hospital but didn't want to worry me. He has herniated disks in his lower back, but not to worry because he is out of the hospital now and will receive a second opinion when he gets back to the states next year. Yep, he has definitely grown up on me, and not just because his 21st birthday is today. I have a 21-year-old son today! How did that happen?!?! I sure do miss him like stupid crazy....

December 10, 2015 (Facebook post)
A few prayer requests: I have a second interview this morning for a position that I am praying I am offered. Alex also has a few important doctor appointments over the next few days. So far, he hasn't needed insulin but it has been borderline. We are believing the endocrinologist will have great news for us. We will also find out the weight bearing status on his arm. Jackson has an appointment today with the school administrators to discuss his needs in returning to school. Jacob has an appointment on the sixteenth to discuss removing the cast from his leg. Please keep the prayers coming!

December 10, 2015 (Facebook post)
After my interview this morning I was told they were interviewing seven other candidates and would let me know soon which candidate they chose. I was worried just a little because I felt lead to tell them about the accident and

what our family has been through. This could have been perceived as a possible hindrance to an employer. However, within two hours of leaving the interview, I was called and offered the job! I start on December twenty-first. Thank you to everyone who prayed! Once again God showed up at just the right time!!

I knew with P.J. leaving I would have to find a full-time job and quickly. I simply wouldn't be able to sustain my store as well as pay all the household expenses by myself. The debt that that would have been placed upon my shoulders would be substantial. The first job I interviewed for offered me the position. I loved the company and the people who managed it. It was a small-town, family-owned-and-operated business. God has a way of giving us exactly what we need at exactly the time we need it. I would have to be able to provide for Alex and me on my own. Now I would be able to.

December 13, 2015 (Facebook post)
The boys had fun seeing the lights at Jellystone. It only took about two hours to get in (sarcasm)...I bet they will sleep good tonight!

We did our best to pretend that everything was normal for the boys. We had just all gotten home from the hospital, and it was extremely unfair for them to come home and everything be different. You could cut the tension in our home with a knife. They should have been worried about healing and going back to school after such a long time away, not why their parents were fighting all the time.

December 14, 2015 (Facebook post)
Update: Alex saw the Endocrinologist and Orthopedic Surgeon today. His arm is still broke, but he was able to finally get the non-weight bearing status lifted and can start therapy. We are definitely starting to make progress now!

The endocrinologist said he does not need insulin currently unless absolutely necessary. We will just monitor it daily. However, he believes that at some point in Alex's life that he will be insulin dependent. Good thing we believe that God has healed Alex completely and totally, and don't believe the doctors report! Alex has follow up labs on Wednesday so please pray that all of his numbers are where they need to be. Thanks prayer warriors!

December 20, 2015 (Facebook post)

I wish my Nannie was here. I can hear her voice, "Lucille, you can never follow your heart. It will always lie to you." I know she would have told me, "I told you so" but then she would have set to work on mending my broken heart. I miss her every single day, but some days it is almost unbearable.

My Nannie was hesitant when P.J. and I married. She loved my husband, but she worried about me raising his children and still ending up alone. She had been in one bad relationship after another and didn't think the outcome would go well for me. She trusted my decision and supported me. She always did. But I could also remember the conversations I had with her, and her words would play over and over in my head. She had been afraid I would end up alone after helping him raise his children, and now her words were proving to be true.

C.C. and Her Grandmother Erma Jean

December 21, 2015 (Facebook post)

I am sorry that I have not updated sooner on the boys' progress. Jackson started back to school a week ago and loves it! Of course, he got in trouble his first day back, but it wouldn't have been normal if he hadn't! Jacob is now boot and cast free! He is still limping and has some healing left to do, but we are almost there! We received a call from Alex's doctor that they need to see him immediately to discuss his lab results. His appointment is tomorrow so please pray. We are ready to move forward on his progress, and a bad report just isn't in the agenda. Thanks for following our story and for everything that you have done! Just so you know, you guys rock! By the way...started my new job today and I LOVED it!!!

December 22, 2015 (Facebook post)

Our Christmas tree this year is small and sits on a table. Mainly because there was no room for a normal sized tree with Jackson's wheelchair. But, if anything, I have learned through this not to sweat the small stuff. Who cares how big our tree is? The most important thing is that all of our boys are alive, and here to celebrate Christmas. Plus, I won't have to worry about taking a bunch of decorations down in a few days!

December 27, 2015 (Facebook post)

Some days are worse than others. Even when you do everything right, they still suck. But today, my son came to church with me. Today, Alex and P.J.'s boys live, and today that's enough to make me smile...

Things reached an all-time low between P.J. and me. I had already made the decision to file for a divorce and had consulted an attorney. There was simply no way I would be able to continue to try to fight for a marriage that he obviously didn't want. My good friend talked me into talking to another guy via text message. Something to pass the time and help me get through what I was going through. At first, I refused emphatically. Then the devil swooped in and whispered in my ear, "He did it and is still doing it. Why should you stay faithful to your vows when he obviously didn't? It will make you feel better and he deserves to feel how he's made you feel." So, I began to text him. It didn't take me long to know that there was simply no way I would ever be able to go through with meeting him. I knew that to do so would be committing adultery. I couldn't control what my husband did, but I could control what I did. I decided to confess to my husband what I had done and explained to him that I was hurting. I needed to move on. I had finally accepted defeat. I even told him he could take whatever he wanted to from the marriage so long as he just left me alone. I couldn't spend another day fighting with him. I was emotionally spent.

December 29, 2015 (Facebook post)

Many of you know me well enough to know that I am not okay. Life doesn't always turn out the way we think it will. But I know that in this too God didn't bring me here to leave me here. I WILL be okay, and I will come out on the other side of this. So I ask all of you again, for me this time, to pray. Everyone thinks I am so strong, and I will be again, but right now I am not. I could use any prayers you are willing to send my way.

December 29, 2015 (Facebook post)

Update: Alex saw the Gastrointestinal specialist today. He said that according to Alex's labs, Alex shouldn't have survived. He is now being sent to a cardiologist and we have been told it could be up to a year for him to completely heal. Please continue to pray for Alex, for complete healing of his body and mind.

This is just another example of how prayer makes all of the difference. The reason Alex survived is because God heard and answered all of our prayers!!!

Until this point, we simply didn't know why Alex's cholesterol had been so high, even as a younger teenager. We knew that he had received internal injuries during the wreck, which had inflamed his pancreas, but he was too young for this to be the cause of his pancreatitis. We finally had an answer. He was diagnosed with Hypolipoproteinemia Type 4. His body basically overproduced triglycerides. At one point, his numbers reached over 2000. The normal range is below 150. This is a genetic disease that typically passes down directly from a father or a mother. In our case, his father and I didn't have it. Alex just happened to be in that very small percentage of people who inherited it from a grandparent. Since his father and I really were not sure who our fathers were, we also had no way of knowing what our medical history was or whom Alex had received it from.

To finally have an answer felt amazing. Although Hypolipoproteinemia Type IV can be life threatening and would completely alter the course of Alex's life, it was also something that we could treat now that we had an answer. Almost a year later, Alex would once again be fighting for his life in the ICU due to diabetic ketoacidosis. The amazing doctors at Vanderbilt finally discovered the right medication to treat his Hyperlipoproteinemia Type IV, and he has been so much healthier since. Due to the damage to his pancreas, he also developed diabetes. As time progressed, he required less and less insulin. Alex is now a healthy teenager and doesn't need insulin anymore. For the first time ever, his labs are perfect.

January 6, 2016 (Facebook post)

All things work together for the good. Had the wreck not happened, we may have possibly never known that Alex had a heart condition. The doctor said he wouldn't have lived but maybe a few years, and we wouldn't have known why he had suddenly died. We now have a chance to find a specialist that can provide treatment options for him. Even better, we can specifically pray for God to heal him and now know what to ask for. I BELIEVE with everything I have that God didn't bring us to this place to leave us here. Alex WILL be healed, and Jackson WILL walk again. Just wait and see how good our GOD is!!!

CHAPTER 14

*Pray always. Pray in the Spirit. Pray about
everything in every way you know how! And
keeping all this in mind, pray on behalf of
God's people. Keep on praying feverishly,
and be on the lookout until evil has been stayed.*

EPHESIANS 6:18 THE VOICE

ONE NIGHT, AS I lay in the bed pouring my heart out to God, He whispered, "Pray for him." Let me tell you, that was the last thing I wanted to do! Kick him, yes. Take a Bible and smack him upside the head with it? Yep! Pray for him? Not a chance! But something happens spiritually inside us when we become utterly and emotionally spent. We find God. It is there, in our moments of desperation, that we realize He was there all along. He is the ONLY one we can turn to. Not our family. Not our friends. God and God alone. Only He has the answers to give us. I knew that I couldn't fix this. I could not change my husband's heart. There were no words for me to say that would make him understand how much I loved him and our family. I would not be able to love him through this, no matter how much I tried. But God could.

So I began praying for him. At first, I had to dig deep to find the words to pray. Slowly, my prayers became more heartfelt. It was in those hours of prayer day after day that I discovered that I could forgive my husband, whether we stayed in our marriage or not. I did love him and wanted what was best for him, even if that meant letting him and our boys go. God started to unravel for me my husband's heart and what he was going through. I was able to understand how our marriage had gotten to this point. I saw my husband's weaknesses and fears. I saw the pain he was going through and how alone he too must have felt during the accident and afterward. These were revelations that I would never have been able to come to on my own. By nature, I can be the most stubborn and unforgiving person on the planet. Forgiveness does not come easy for me, but thankfully I serve a God who forgives all, and with His help, I can too.

I was at my new job just before New Year's Eve when my husband randomly sent me a text saying, "I hope you have a good day." My heart almost leaped out of my chest. What did this mean? Do I text him back? Ignore it? He had finally left me alone, and now he was sending me a text message being nice. I decided to text him back telling him to have a good day as well. I would prefer things to end with us still able to be kind to each other. What I didn't realize at the time was he had already broken things off with the other girl and was trying for a reconciliation. He decided to text me, and, depending on my response, he would know whether he had a chance or not. Because my response was nice, he decided to go for it. Of course, I was completely oblivious to his motives. I was just happy that we could communicate without screaming at each other.

Over the course of the next week, we slowly began to speak to each other as friends. He apologized again and again for what he had done and the way he had hurt me. The turning point for him, he told me later, was when he became so angry he threw something at me. He realized he had become this person he didn't recognize anymore. He started doing a lot of praying and self-reflection. He began to really think about what he wanted his future to look like, and he couldn't see me not being there by his side.

It took several months, but our marriage began to change. Every day isn't perfect. We still have arguments and days when we simply don't want to deal with each other. But we also love each other differently. It's not how we imagined love to be, but we love each other in the ways that matter. I have learned to forgive a lot quicker instead of holding on to my anger for days on end. I have learned to communicate more about my feelings, unlike before, when I would just bottle everything up inside. He has learned to accept that I will never be extremely affectionate. It simply isn't in my nature to be so. We both discovered that love isn't a feeling, but an action. When things get hard, we learn exactly what this means. After the accident, my husband and I were 100 percent focused on our children. There was little left over for each other at the end of each day. And instead of pulling closer to each other, we pulled completely apart. Our actions didn't line up with what our love for each other should have been. We should have been acting out of love, even when we didn't have room to "feel" love for each other. We now chose to do things differently.

C.C. and P.J.

January 7, 2016 (Facebook post)

Thanks so much for all of the birthday wishes! It was a wonderful day and all of your comments made it that much more special :) P.J. sent me flowers to work then I came home to this huge surprise!!!

January 9, 2016 (Facebook post)

Urgent: Please pray for Alex. Someone t-boned him at an intersection. He says his car is totaled but he is okay. We are on our way there now from Murfreesboro. Please pray that God gives him comfort and that there are no injuries he isn't aware of.

January 9, 2016 (Facebook post)

Update: Alex is sore and says he is never driving again, but he is okay. He is obviously shaken up as he just started driving a few weeks ago and started a new job 3 days ago at Pizza Hut delivering pizza. So now he has lost his car and says he isn't going to be able to drive for work anymore. I am disappointed that one of the officers was rude to me and never bothered asking Alex if he was okay or if he needed medical attention. I would have thought that was normal protocol, especially when he wasn't at fault for the accident. We are so thankful that the impact was on the back drivers side. Had it been a few feet different in either direction the outcome would have been much different. God was once again watching over our family. The devil is hard at work trying to destroy us, but God has already defeated him. Y'all just wait and see, Alex is going to do great things!

My husband and I were on our first actual date since the accident. We were finally back to where we had been well before the accident and were having such a wonderful evening. On our way back home from dinner, I had a strange feeling come over me, and I was immediately concerned for Alex and said a silent prayer of protection over him. I couldn't shake it and told my husband that I was worried about him driving in the rain. Alex had just recently started driving again and had taken a job at Pizza Hut. It was only his third day on the job. He was happier than I had seen him in months. Everything was going perfect. My husband and I had finally come together again, and it was better than ever. Alex was finally starting to live life as any other normal teenager would. Life was as perfect as it could be.

As we were discussing our fear for him driving again and how we would have to have faith, my phone rang. It was Alex. I knew that he had been in another accident before my ear touched my phone. I had so many thoughts running through my mind in just a few short seconds before I heard his voice. God told me, "It is going to be okay. Have faith, because I have this too under control." I knew this was going to be another trial to overcome. I also knew that God would be there with us through it all. Alex explained that he was turning left at a green light when someone ran a red light and T-boned the car we had just purchased for him. He said he had already called the police, and they were on the way. He was okay, just very sore and shaken up. He didn't know if the other driver was okay because they didn't stop.

While driving to the scene, my husband and I talked about how calm we were. Before the "big accident," as we now call it, we would have been terrified. Now, we unfortunately had experience with this. Once we arrived on the scene, we discovered that the other driver did eventually pull over farther down the road. She explained to the officers that she didn't realize the light was red due to the rain until it was too late to stop. One of the officers recognized Alex and asked him if he was in the other wreck with his brothers, and Alex responded yes. This completely shook up the woman who had hit Alex, and she apologized over and over. It was simply an accident. Just like the first one.

Unfortunately, this one had worse consequences for Alex than the first one did. To this day, he still has a fear of driving. He doesn't drive in the rain unless absolutely necessary and will plan his day around the weather forecast. Of course, this meant he would no longer be able to deliver pizzas and had to give up his job. He would have panic attacks just from riding in a vehicle, especially a car. We would have to replace his vehicle much later with a small SUV. The only people he would ever let drive him from that day forward were his dad and me. He was later diagnosed with severe PTSD. I believe that it was just too many accidents in such a short time. There's nothing like realizing that you have zero control of your life in such a dramatic way. None of us do, even if we think we do. Alex, however, had learned this lesson abruptly and severely. This was the third time in less than five months that he had almost lost his life. His fear is something that I am sure he will have to deal with for the rest of his life. I remember one day asking God, "Why does it have to be so hard for him? Why does he have to go through all of this? It just isn't fair!" God led me to this poem:

When God wants to drill a man,
And thrill a man,
And skill a man
To play his noblest part;
When He yearns with all His heart
To create so great and bold a man
That all the world shall be amazed,
Watch His methods, watch His ways!
How He ruthlessly perfects
Whom He royally elects!
How He hammers him and hurts him,
And with mighty blows converts him
Into trial shapes of clay witch

Only God understands;
While his tortured heart is crying
And he lifts beseeching hands!
How He bends but never breaks
When his good he undertakes;
How He uses whom He chooses,
And with every purpose fuses him;
Be every act induces him
To try His splendor out—
God Knows what He's about.
~ Author Unknown

I realized that this was Alex's journey. God uses everything for His purpose. Everything that Alex goes through only makes him stronger. Wiser. It builds his faith in God. I have always known since Alex was a little boy that he would do great things for God. He was prophesied over as a young boy by our pastor that he would do great things for the Kingdom of God and would someday preach the Word. Our faith is built in the trials that we endure in life. How can we truly have faith if nothing ever goes wrong in our lives? Unless we have been at the bottom of the very bottom, we can't truly know what it is like to cry out to God out of desperation and hope. Alex almost lost his life, and during that process he found God in a way that many people never have the chance to experience. He knew, beyond all shadow of a doubt, that he was alive because of God. Every person has his or her own cross to bear. This was Alex's. I couldn't change it. I couldn't make it better for him. I could not heal his heart. I could not alleviate his fears. As a mother, this was hard to accept. Moms are supposed to fix the boo-boos and make them better. In all reality, only God can do that. All I could do going forward was to love him through everything he would have to go through, physically and emotionally. I could pray for him. I could be there for him. But God would have to be the One to restore him, not me.

January 10, 2016 (Facebook post)

I am sure some people think I must be crazy or naïve in my faith. Because from the worlds perspective, only a crazy person would continue to find the good in the tragedies of our lives these last few months. Am I afraid? Yep. Did my heart take a flying leap when I got that call last night? Sure did. Will Alex drive again and me not be afraid? Yes. Because this I know for certain, God has and will always be in control. That doesn't mean that the outcome is always good or what we want. I am thankful that God chose again to protect my son and let him live. But faith is grown in the hard times, when all seems lost and we don't understand why life is so hard. I don't have to like the circumstances, and trust me…it has not been a bag of lollipops. Getting the diagnosis and Alex being in another accident in the same week??? Yes, there are times when I want to throw my hands up in the air and scream at God at the top of my lungs. Yet, I know that this is when God wants us to trust Him the most. This is when He reveals his grace, healing and mercy. He has a plan and purpose, and I think we should all jump on the crazy train and trust in Him.

January 11, 2016 (Facebook post)

Seeing both of the cars side by side today, I am reminded how blessed I truly am. I know it seems like we have had the worst luck imaginable, but in all reality, I see it as being blessed beyond measure because God just keeps proving that He is watching over our boys!

THE DEVIL KEEPS TRYING, BUT GOD KEEPS WINNING!

Both Cars Side by Side

January 21, 2016 (Facebook post)

I am once again asking for prayers for Alex. He was walking up the stairs this morning and his knee (the one that has a metal rod in it from the broken femur) popped and he is unable to walk or put any pressure on it. We are waiting to hear from his orthopedic surgeon at Vanderbilt to see what we need to do.

A year later, Alex would indeed have knee surgery because of injuries from the second accident. The day of the surgery, he was up and walking!

—⁂—

As P.J. and C.C. sat around a bonfire at our home with us, we heard the back door open. There was Jackson, rolling himself through the doorway onto the back deck. They had come to celebrate my husband's birthday with us and a few friends that Saturday in February. Jackson was done playing video games inside and wanted to come out to the fire with us. I watched my husband and P.J. carefully lift Jackson and carry him down the steps in his wheelchair. P.J. then helped him wheel through the yard to his place at the fire between himself and C.C. I remember thinking how deeply Jackson's life had changed over the past several months, and my heart weighed heavy. Then Jackson reached across and tried to steal P.J.'s drink, which then brought on a scuffling match between father and son. They swiped at each other playfully, P.J. laughing and Jackson giggling and taunting his dad. At that moment, I saw C.C. roll her eyes slightly and laugh as she watched them. It was then that I realized that though life had changed dramatically for all of them, they had remained the same. They were still the same P.J., C.C., Justin, Alex, Jacob, Josh, and Jackson. They were just stronger and closer as a family. Closer to one another, and closer to God.

Melissa Wray, P.J.'s sister-in-law

—⚏—

January 22, 2016 (Facebook post)
I keep an overnight bag packed at all times for the hospital. I wasn't surprised to receive the call yesterday from Alex that we had to rush back to Vanderbilt, and I have an army of medical professionals stored in my phone.

I have heard myself say over and over that Alex has the worst luck. If it could happen, it will.

On the way to the hospital yesterday God reminded me that he told Alex he would have four quarters to go through before his part of this journey was over, so why did I expect the doctor to give us a bad report? Yes, his symptoms indicated the worst, but God had made a promise, and He does not lie.

Expectations. I have expected the bad to happen. Prepared and braced myself. I have spoken negative over Alex continuously, without realizing it. I somehow forgot along the way that my words have the power of life and death. When we assume the bad will happen, inevitably it will.

I'm reminded that I will never be perfect, only He is. I have a lot of growing left to do, in every single area of my life. Because that is what life is all about. To learn, change, and evolve.

March 29, 2016 (Blog Post)

I love the drive home from school every day. It is just me and Jackson. He uses this time to talk to me about things on his mind. Sometimes, it's as simple as a question about the calorie content in chocolate milk. Others, he allows me glimpse into his personal thoughts about his injury and the changes his life has endured since becoming paralyzed.

The other day he told me that sometimes people can be mean. Yes Jackson, they sure can! A person that he plays online video games with was calling him gay. I've been told that people can be very hateful and use foul language on these online gaming systems, but our choice as parents has never been to shelter our children. He then proceeded to tell me that it's okay because he has a friend online that is also good to him, "He takes care of me and watches after me." Jackson told me that he even told his friend that he was now paralyzed. This may not seem like a big deal to some, but it was the very first time I have ever heard Jackson refer to himself as being paralyzed. And he told a perfect stranger that he's never laid eyes on. I believe this was Jackson's way of testing the waters so to speak. He was able to confide in this person because he doesn't know him personally, but trusted him because he has shown Jackson kindness. Jackson is a very quiet little boy and doesn't share his feeling and thoughts freely. We only get small glimpses into what he is thinking.

You would think from the outside looking in this is something we talk about all the time. We don't. We decided to go back to our normal lives, in every possible way. We don't pretend that he isn't paralyzed. We just simply allow Jackson to process it as it comes. It is his life that has been altered. It is up to him to decide how he wants to feel about it. How he allows it to affect him. Yes, as parents we push him to accomplish things whether he is in a chair or standing on two feet. Yes, we teach him that he can do anything that he wants. We must make him do physical therapy, learn how to understand his body and warning signs to watch for. It is a part of our daily lives now, but it doesn't define us and how we choose to live.

We have a long way to go, physically and emotionally. He completely shuts down when he is around other kids in wheelchairs or is around someone talking about his paralysis. I know there is a level of acceptance that he has to work through. But Jackson is the strongest kid I have ever met, and he will do it…but it will be in his own time, as it should be.

March 31, 2016 (Blog Post)

Sometimes God puts things on my heart to share with others. My purpose since the beginning has been to share our story and allow God to be visible through my life. I believe that this is something that I needed to share.

I have seen first-hand how social media can make some people seem like they have the most perfect life in the world. I don't want anyone to ever think that I am the most positive uplifting person they will ever meet. I have never been that person and in fact, shared very early on that I was the most glass half empty person you would have ever met before the accident.

I have days when the enormity of the accident and the changes our lives have taken are overwhelming. I have moments when my heart skips a beat thinking about all that Jackson has lost by becoming paralyzed. I have what ifs. What if I hadn't wanted to surprise the boys by redecorating their room? What if P.J. and I had gone to pick them up from their grandparents? What if their grandmother had brought them home instead of us needing to ask Alex to pick them up?

There are days when I have to-do lists for my to-do lists and I want to throw my hands up in the air and cry mercy. I am only able to work part-time now as Jackson needs to be taken to school and picked up early every day. I have weeks when I feel like I might as well rent a hotel room next to Vanderbilt Children's Hospital because I spend so much time there. My husband and I have had one date night since the accident. Yes, you read that right. We have been unable to find anyone who is willing to spend time with Jackson. In fact, I have been unable to work this week except for four hours as the kids are home for spring break and I have had to stay home with them.

Does it sound like I am complaining? Perhaps I am some. And that is the point. This hasn't been an easy adjustment for any of us. No, I am not perfect. Yes, I have moments when I actually consider running away like a child throwing a temper tantrum. Yes, I believe that God has a purpose and a plan for our boys. I absolutely believe that someday Jackson WILL walk again. I know with every fiber of my being that Alex is meant to share the gospel and bring others into the Kingdom of God. I also know that God has used me by sharing our story to bring others into His Kingdom, to encourage others and give them hope.

What I hope that I am expressing is that just because I have faith doesn't mean that I am not human. We all have emotions that we must process. We make mistakes. We are allowed moments of self-doubt. I also think us women are allowed a pity party every now and then. What really matters at the end of the day is if you allow those moments to define you.

When I become overwhelmed with grief for Jackson, God reminds me how blessed we are to have Jackson alive and still here with us. To be around Jackson is to know happiness and peace. When I think about what Alex has had to go through, God reminds me that He is making Alex strong. He is allowing Alex to walk this journey so that he will be able to share what he has overcome and give him relevance with those he will someday be able to help. And on days when I am having a pity party and I think I couldn't get any more tired than

I already am, God reminds me just how blessed I truly am. I am a work in progress. I have come so far since the accident and have learned so much, but He still has to work a little extra harder on me.

It is okay to have doubts. It is okay to have moments of frustration. News Flash: you don't have to be perfect! Just don't allow those moments to define your life. Use those times to seek God even more and allow Him to be the light in the darkness.

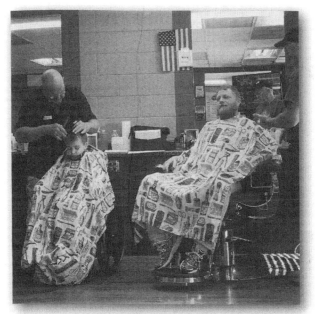

Jackson's First Haircut after the Accident

April 4, 2016 (Blog Post)

We spent the day cleaning up the yard, pulling weeds and getting ready for summer. I haven't tended to a garden in two years. I was so busy with work that I didn't "have" time to. The reality is, I prioritized responsibility first and forgot to tend to myself. I love being outdoors and do my best thinking pulling weeds and deadheading plants. I have decided this year that I must learn to do things for myself too, and gardening is something that soothes my soul.

I tried to convince Jackson to come outside with everyone, but the problem with that is his brothers were riding bikes, and of course he can't do a lot of what they want to do outside. Before you scream at me for using the word can't, the reality is there are things that he is simply not able to do. He must build strength first.

As parents, we struggle with balance. We want to keep Jackson happy, and sometimes it is at his brothers' expense because they are talked into doing what he wants to do. His brothers are awesome and tend to want to keep him happy too, but sometimes it's difficult for them. An example, Jacob wanted to have his birthday party at the Bouncy House. Jackson would not have been able to do all the things his brothers were doing, so we chose to let Jacob have a bonfire and sleep over instead. It's a check and balance. All parents understand this, it is just at a new level we are coming to learn.

As I was outside surveying our progress, I noticed Jackson's tricycle behind the shed. My heart immediately stopped and I was overwhelmed with panic as I tried to remember if Jackson had learned to ride a bike without training wheels. Suddenly, I realize he hadn't. Another thing that he won't have the chance to remember doing before the accident.

I sometimes wonder how much he will actually remember. Will he remember how it feels to run? Will he remember playing in the waves at the beach? Dragging our feet in the sand to write his name? Will he remember hiking with his brothers and walking through the creeks?

My heart grows heavy with thoughts like this. I believe it is normal as a parent to learn to accept what can and can't be. To process what he must go through and will go through. These are thoughts that he too has and will have. Answers he will need. But as I am sitting and contemplating this, he comes outside with his oldest brother and starts practicing casting a fishing real. God reminded me in that moment that there are so many things he can and will do. He has a family that loves him, and brothers that will always protect him and look after him. Despite all that we perceive he has lost, he is so very blessed.

April 4, 2016 (Blog Post)

My husband told me several days ago that Jackson asked him if I would get mad if he called me mom. I knew he had been thinking about something along these lines by the questions he had been asking lately. I should start by explaining why Jackson would be contemplating such a thing. We have had full custody of my husband's three boys for over four years. Jackson doesn't remember a time that he didn't live with us and our 13-year-old has been calling me mom for a couple of years. After my husband and I married, I explained to them that I was not their mom and didn't ever want to take her place. My name is C.C. and that is what they should call me. When Jacob first started calling me mom I was concerned. After giving it much thought, I realized that he was old enough to make that choice on his own and needed me to fill the void that he was feeling by his mom not being in his life consistently.

I am explaining this because so many people simply don't know that our youngest boys are not mine biologically. I treat them as if they are my own. In my heart, they are. When my husband and I married, we said vows not just to each other, but to our children as well. The wedding ceremony was more about showing them through action that we were combining our family together and making commitments to each other, not just between husband and wife, but most importantly, to them. If you have read any of my previous posts, you will remember that after the accident Alex pleaded with the paramedics to help his brothers.

We are not a blended family. We are family.

I believe that being a mother is about more than just giving birth. Being a mother isn't the name your children call you. Being a mother is shown by actions. It is a verb. It means taking them to doctor appointments, making them do their homework and brush their teeth. It means teaching them right and wrong. To hold the door open for women and lift the toilet seat when they use the bathroom (let's be real here). It means sleepless nights when they are sick. Hugs when they need comfort and discipline when they choose to not follow rules. I treat my husband's boys as I would my own, in every possible way. Of course, I want them to love me. I want their approval. But I will not and have never been afraid to do what I know in my heart is best for them. My philosophy has always been that they can grow up to hate me and that is okay with me as long as they grow up to be great men. I love them too much to do anything less.

As we were on our way to Vanderbilt Children's Hospital today, Jackson finally decided to discuss the idea of calling me mom with me. Thank God my husband gave me advance notice because I probably would have cried all the way to Nashville and the whole conversation would have been a catastrophe. I explained to him that I would not be upset in the least and that it was his choice to make. I believe that he will continue to call me C.C., simply out of habit. To be honest, it doesn't really matter. What did matter was that by his question I know that he knows that I love him as a mother should. He knows that even though I am not his biological mother, I have treated him as my son. And at the end of the day, whatever he chooses to call me, that is all that matters.

P.S. I know that this is personal and some would perhaps wonder why I choose to share it. There are several reasons…First, this blog is about my life and raising our boys after such a tragic event in our lives. Second, I am an open book. I value truth and can't expect to receive it unless I am willing to give it. Lastly, life is too short to worry about what others think or being afraid to step on toes, so I don't.

April 11, 2016 (Blog Post)

I had not seen my grandmother's tombstone since it was installed two weeks after the accident (she died a few months before). Nor had I visited my grandfather. There wasn't time the first several months after the accident. It is also a long drive and something I was afraid to face alone, but God had placed it on my heart in the last week to finally make the time to do it. On Sunday, I knew I could no longer put it off.

I don't find comfort in visiting gravesite's, as some do. I remember a conversation my Nannie and I once had about visiting Drew's gravesite after the tombstone was installed. He was my 18-year-old cousin who tragically died a few years ago in a car accident. She found comfort visiting it, I didn't. And here I was on a beautiful Sunday afternoon, staring at hers. Faced with the reality of time from that conversation to the present and all that had happened in the last year. Forced to confront the fact that one of my worst fears had come to pass. My Nannie, who was my best friend, was really gone.

I cried for all I was worth. I cried because my heart aches from missing her. I cried for what my boys have been through. I cried for what I have been through. A huge part of me wanted to suck up the tears and run. But I knew that wasn't why God had led me there. It was finally time to accept that she was really gone. It was time to deal with the emotions of everything my family has been through since the accident. It was finally time to grieve.

—∞—

Jesus had holes in his hands and feet.

Jackson

—∞—

As I was leaving after visiting with my grandfather, he told me that he had prayed the previous night for God to give him a good day. I was the answer to his prayer and God's miracle for him. You see, God knew a week ago that he would need a visit from family to remind him that he isn't alone and that he is loved. God knew my heart couldn't carry the weight of hurt I had been carrying around anymore. He knew from the minute he placed it on my heart a week ago.

Sometimes God asks us to do things that we know will ultimately cause us pain. We don't understand the reason, but He does. If God has asked you to do something, just remember that He doesn't bring us to it to leave us there in that place of pain and hurt. He will bring you through it, to a place of healing and restoration. You can trust in Him.

April 15, 2016 (Blog Post)

I will be honest and admit that I was really worried about Jackson's field day at school. Jackson, of course, was completely ready and beyond excited about it. We picked out the Powerades he wanted to take and his clothes the evening before. In his mind, he was going to be able to do everything. It is sometimes hard to imagine how his 7-year-old mind processes things. He has never seen what he can't do, only how he CAN do it.

It didn't take him long to realize just how different this day would be from the two other field days he had participated in before. Jackson has always handled his emotions better than even most adults. He processes his emotions slowly and has very little tells to clue you in to what he is thinking. He became quiet and put his head in his lap.

As a parent, it is hard to watch I know what he is feeling. What he is thinking. And I can't change it. He has been invited to birthday parties that involve physical activity. I hadn't wanted to face it so we didn't go. Jackson runs headlong into everything. I was the one scared. I knew eventually we would have to face this. It was inevitable. And when he whispered to me in his low voice, "I wish I could walk." All I could say is, "Me too baby."

When someone handed him the first ribbon just for participating, the look on his face broke my heart. I know they were trying to help. They were trying to include him and make him feel special. He saw it for what it was. A ribbon he didn't earn. I was torn between wanting him to succeed in each event in any way possible, and wanting to push him to earn the ribbon himself. After the egg race, he put his head down and whispered to me, "I am a bad boy because I cheated." Even though he was told to hold the egg while someone pushed his chair, he felt like he had cheated by doing so.

Finally, he won a ribbon on his own. Of course, he had to participate in a special way, but this ribbon he DESERVED. Even though he struggled during each race with what he couldn't do, he still participated in every single one that he was able. This kid doesn't let anything stop him. Yes, he struggles sometimes accepting what is. But, he still pushes forward, despite it all.

Although my first reaction when he wanted to go into the bouncy house was to worry about how it could be done and how his body would respond, I quickly replied, "Let's do it!" So, we both went into the bouncy house together! He had a blast and the smile on his face was worth my now very sore muscles (they need these things in gyms for adults because it is a definite workout, let me tell ya).

I am very thankful that Jackson goes to a school that allows him to try to do everything he can. For a teacher that pushes him. And for an assistant that loves on him when we aren't there to do so.

And by the time we were on our way home, he was proud of all the awards he had, even those he didn't earn himself. As he told his brother Joshua with a huge smile on his face, "They gave me all of these ribbons. It's the good thing about being paralyzed."

April 18, 2016 (Blog Post)

I love my conversations with Jackson when it is just me and him in the truck. I never know just what we may talk about. Sometimes, it is a funny story, other times it is just a million of other random questions as kids are subject to do.

Today, he talked to me about his trip to Heaven.

I always knew there was more to share than he was ready to talk about the first time he told me he saw Jesus the day of the accident. Today he wanted to talk to me about the details of his trip.

He said that he went up the stairs to Heaven. When he got toward the top he started to have a good feeling all over his body, and that is when he saw Jesus. Although he didn't have to talk with his mouth, Jesus told him that he was going to be paralyzed but that he was going to be okay.

He also spoke about how in Heaven you could instantly think of things but before you could finish the thought it appeared. Things were instant in Heaven, and he knew immediately that being paralyzed meant him being in a wheelchair.

I believe there was more with the experience of "instant thoughts" that make things appear, but he isn't ready to speak about it, and I don't push him. He will share it when he is ready.

He said that coming back to his body was also instant. He was in Heaven one minute and he opened his eyes to the paramedics walking with him on the stretcher the next.

We then talked about how blessed he is that God gave him "another life" as he calls it. I am the one blessed, because I get to share my life with this awesome kid!

I am sharing Jackson's story because I know this is something that God has asked me to do. I pray that his story touches others who need it. If someone was unsure about God and the truth of His Word, I pray Jackson's experience helps them to see just how good God is. If they feel alone, this helps them to know that they are never alone. There is a God who loves them and one day they will be reunited with lost loved ones.

Help me share Jackson's story by sharing it with others. Tell it to your friends and family. Share it on Facebook and Twitter. Help others know that yes, there is a God and oh man He is GOOD!

—꙳—

There were a lot of kids in Heaven. Some had wings.
Some didn't. They were playing and having fun.

Jackson

—m—

May 4, 2016 (Blog Post)

Menopause. Seriously?!?! I am thirty-eight years old, and according to the doctor…in full-blown menopause. I thought the doctor had to be wrong. Or at least making a not-so-funny joke. Nope, the second labs confirmed the diagnosis.

I shouldn't be surprised. I mean c'mon, my body was surely going to have some type of protest after the last year. Losing my Nannie, then the accident and subsequent months in the hospital would take its toll on anyone. Also, did y'all know the IRS audited us three days after the wreck?? Nope, not kidding. And they didn't care that we were in the hospital with our children or that they might die. Carla and Barbra from Bookkeeping Plus was such a blessing and took over everything AND made several trips to Vanderbilt. Did I mention that her and her team put in untold amounts of hours and didn't even charge us??? Needless to say, if menopause is the worst of it, then I am fortunate.

At first, I wasn't going to talk about this but with only my closest family and friends. It is kind of embarrassing to admit that I am going through the "change of life" and I am not even forty. That is what older women do, right??? But after thinking about it, I decided I wasn't going to allow my age to define me.

My body has earned the right to go into full-blown menopause at any age! After all, I have birthed two beautiful boys. I have endured levels of stress that most could only begin to imagine. Yet, I am still standing strong. And best of all…I haven't committed a physical assault on anyone!! Plus, I now have the perfect excuse. It isn't my fault, blame it on the menopause!

With Mother's Day just a few days away, I am reminded why I am proud to be a woman. To be a mother. They say being a mother is the hardest job in the world. I absolutely freaking agree!!! It is also the most rewarding thing a woman can ever experience. Yes, we must deal with all the drama of being a woman, including trivial little matters like menopause. But at the end of it all, anything and everything is worth the joy of being a mother. To be a mother, I will embrace menopause and everything else that comes with it.

May 8, 2016 (Blog Post)

Mother's Day: A day that florists prepare to work extra hours fulfilling orders. A day that restaurant owners know that they will be busy with reservations. Jewelry companies advertise giving your mom or wife that special piece of jewelry to "let her know you care."

So many moms hope that on this day her husband and children will suddenly realize how important she is to them. How much she does and sacrifices for them. We hope that somehow, they have had an aha moment and want to surprise us with gifts and acts of appreciation and love. We "drop" hints about ways they can surprise us. We see our friends on Facebook being spoiled with lavish gifts and trips and hope that we too get to show everyone how loved we are.

The truth is, a lot of the time, we end up disappointed.

Being a mother is the most challenging job a person will ever have. And once we become a mother, it is a lifelong sentence. But it is also the most rewarding. Our joy of being a mother doesn't come from gifts or words of appreciation. It doesn't come from a husband that shows his appreciation on a day that is supposed to be celebrated for all that we do. Our joy comes from watching our children grow. The pride we receive when we see them act with love and kindness toward others. When they step out into the world to follow their dreams and act with strength and courage when faced with life's trials and tribulations.

I woke up today and went to church by myself. I picked up lunch and brought it to them. I took a nap, which I never do but decided that

I was going to take the time for me today. I didn't get lavish gifts or words of praise. After the year we had, I had hoped that my family would suddenly want to show me how much they loved me…but they didn't. Next year will be the same. After a little while of feeling sorry for myself, I remembered that Mother's Day is a commercial holiday. Our appreciation doesn't come from gifts or material items. It doesn't even come from our husbands or our children. Not in the way that we sometimes think that it should.

I hope that all of those moms who feel unappreciated today know that they are loved and valued. Your value isn't in the gifts you receive on Mother's Day. It doesn't come from a husband who appreciates your worth. Your value is in doing the hardest job imaginable. Every time you have prayed and cried for your child. Those times when they were sick or hurt and you wished more than your next breath that you could take it away from them. For every sacrifice you have made so that they could have what they needed. God chose you to shape the next generation. He chose you to be a mother. What better honor is there than that? That ladies, is your value.

May 12, 2016 (Blog Post)

I have spent the past couple of days planning for Jackson's surgery and Alex's graduation. How can one do both emotionally and not be a basket case? The answer is simple: by the grace of God.

Nine months ago, our boys were life flighted to Vanderbilt. We didn't have time to clean the house, make sure the laundry was done, the pets were taken care of or to pack bags. In fact, for several days we only had the clothes on our backs. After multiple surgeries and several months, we were all finally home together. This time, Jackson's surgery is planned. We know how long the recovery should take. We are not naive to be oblivious to the possibility of complications. Of course, we are not happy that he must be put to sleep and cut open again, but we don't have a choice. We knew from the beginning that the surgeons were creating surgical hernias that would someday need to be repaired. We didn't care. We wanted him to live. As much as we worry for him, we also know that God is the One in control. I say it all the time, but it is so very true. Since that day on the side of the road I have learned that He is always in control, not me. It isn't ideal for my husband and me to miss a week or two more of work, but God provided for us before, and I must believe He will do so again.

While planning to be in the hospital with Jackson, I have also been planning for Alex's graduation. I still can't believe he is old enough to graduate. He is my baby. He has had to overcome so many obstacles this year to make this happen. More than most adults ever experience in a lifetime. I am so very proud of who he has become. I was amazed at the strength he had during and after the accident. His love for his brothers and people in general. His heart is so very pure and true. Last week he met with Pastor Randy and I could see God working and putting everything together. He has a purpose and I know that he will do mighty things for the Kingdom of God. And so does he. I can't wait to see it!

I am not a basket case because I am blessed. I am blessed that my son, despite every opportunity to throw up his hands and give up, will be graduating high school. I am blessed because our boys are alive, and even though Jackson must have surgery, we know that he will be okay. No matter how bad my day is, I can always look back on what I experienced on August 16, 2015 and find hope and gratitude in God for what He did then and continues to do. He really is an awesome God.

May 20, 2016 (Blog Post)

We made it through surgery without a hitch, although this time was harder for him. Before, one moment he was watching his brother Joshua play a game on his iPad in the backseat of his brother's car, the next he was in the hospital at the mercy of doctors and parents making decisions for him. He didn't have a choice. He didn't have advance notice or time to be afraid.

Every day before his surgery he would look at me once a day and simply say, "Monday." That was his way of letting me know he was scared. Jackson is such a brave kid. I sometimes forget that he is only seven, and that he has the same fears that other kids do too. As we arrived for preop his little body started to shake. His father and I both wanted to load him up in the truck and take off, but we knew we couldn't. I was able to calm him down by crawling in the bed with him and playing games on his iPad. My philosophy has always been to keep yourself busy so that you don't have time to dwell on the bad. So, that's what we did.

Ten minutes before surgery they brought him the "happy" medicine. He was all grins and giggles then. Not a care in the world. The hard part then started for us parents. The waiting.... When your child is in surgery, even if it is considered routine or minor, every second feels like a hundred. This surgery wasn't considered minor. He was having an incisional hernia repaired. There was the danger that his bowels could be injured, and in Jackson's case, he only has half of his bowels left from the damage caused by the seatbelt during the accident.

When the phone finally rings, your heart skips several beats. Is it good news? Bad? Hurry up and answer already!! And if you're not the one taking the call, it's pure torture. You try reading facial expressions to gauge their reaction. Listen to voice inflections. Anything to determine what the listener is hearing. Time stands still. In this case, the news was great. Jackson did well during surgery and was in recovery waking up!

The entire day I didn't feel well but thought it was anxiety and lack of sleep. By the time his surgery was over, there was no doubt that it was more than anxiousness. I was running a fever. We discussed if I should stay or go and decided that at that point I had already exposed Jackson. Remember me crawling into bed with him during preop? By that evening my husband was running a fever and by the next morning Jackson was too. Jacob didn't feel well Sunday evening and had unknowingly given us all the flu. Wonderful, right????? Sometimes, I wonder why things have to be so difficult for us. Surgery was enough to deal with, but now poor Jackson had to deal with having the flu on top of recovering from surgery.

The difference between moms and dads: when moms and the kids are sick at the same time, we still take care of everything. When dads get sick, they can sleep through a nuclear war. So, by the end of the week it is no surprise that everyone else is on the mend and I am still sick. That's just the way it is for us moms. No one ever thinks to take care of us.

This surgery was a monkey on our back. Now, it is done and over with. At some point, Jackson may have to have another hernia repaired, but the doctor thinks it will be a long time from now. He will also have to have spinal surgery to put more rods in his back to combat the Scoliosis. Again, this will hopefully be after his bones have fully matured and several years down the road. For now, Jackson can live life without having this surgery looming over him. We are thankful for that. We are looking forward to him healing and being able to swim this summer.

Did I mention that this kid missed half the school year and still made an A and C on his report card?!? This kid rocks!!!

———— ⚂ ————

CHAPTER 15

Lead me by your truth and teach me, for you are the
God who saves me. All day long I put my hope in you.

PSALM 25:5 NLT

May 22, 2016 (Blog Post)

YESTERDAY WE WERE at the point of taking Jackson back to Vanderbilt. He literally could not stop coughing. I was diagnosed with a sinus infection and was afraid his had turned into one too. Seems like no biggie, but Jackson's lungs are comprised due to his spinal cord injury. A sinus infection and congestion can quickly lead to pneumonia.

Lately, God has reminded me of the faith I used to have. Some of you are thinking, "Used to have?" You see, I believe in laying hands on the sick. I believe in speaking in tongues. I believe in angels and demons. I believe in dancing and shouting and praising the God that has saved me. Some call it Pentecostal. Some may even call it crazy. Somehow along the way I lost it. It's not that I stopped believing, I just lost my fire for God. Let's be honest, we all lose our way at different times in our lives. Something happens and we pull back from God, even without realizing it. It can be something traumatic, like losing someone you love. Or something as simple as being busy in your day to day life.

So, last night as I was desperate for Jackson to feel better, I immediately thought, "I need to ask our friends on Facebook to pray for him." And God said, "You do it." But…it takes lots of prayers! Not just my prayer. It takes an army of prayer warriors. I am a simple mom. My faith isn't enough. "Yes, it is." Don't you love how we sometimes argue with God? Cause surely, I am not the only one who does this, right?!?

So, I did what God told me to do, I laid my hands on him and prayed aloud for his healing. I felt God move through me. Even then, I didn't believe that Jackson would be healed. Not that I don't believe in God, or His miraculous healing. I didn't believe in myself. I didn't believe that my faith was strong enough. That I was good enough for God to use. But God only needs the faith of a mustard seed.

I'm sure you all know where this is going. Jackson WAS healed. And not later. Not the next morning. IMMEDIATELY. This baby had coughed every single minute for two days straight. He coughed the entire time I was praying for him. The minute my hands left his body, he stopped. He has not coughed a single time since.

God had to make me see that yes, I am good enough. I am more than enough. I am His child. My faith, even when it feels small and helpless, is enough, because it isn't me that has the power to do anything. I never did and never will. It is Him. And if we believe in Him, He can and will do amazing things through us. We just have to step out in faith and let Him take the lead.

June 1, 2016 (Blog Post)

I have moaned and groaned about not being able to work. It is definitely an adjustment becoming a stay-at-home mom again, especially when the choice was made for you instead of by you. But lately, God has been reminding me that it is what you choose to do with your time, however it is given, that truly matters. Instead of whining about what I should or could be doing, I should take the time I'm given and use it the best way that I can.

I believe God is using this time to teach me to slow down, and to enjoy the little moments. I have always been the overachiever. All about time management and being productive. I was just running away from fears and doubts. It's hard for God to find you when you are going full speed ahead, all the while complaining about how busy you are and all that must get done. Yet, we allow ourselves to be so busy we forget to make time to spend with our Creator. We are so busy living and complaining about being busy that God ends up on the bottom of our to-do-list, or not on it at all.

After the wreck, everything came into such clear perception in my life. Nothing mattered in that moment except that my children live. Every fear I ever had become nothing in comparison. I wanted the moments back where my kids got on my ever-loving nerves. Y'all know what I'm talking about! I wanted to see a dirty bedroom. I wanted to hear them arguing. I didn't care if the bills were paid. I just wanted my crazy busy life back. It is easy to get busy living life that we forget to actually live. Every day feels like the same from the ones before.

—◦◦◦—

The first time that I heard the story of the wreck—the true story, not bits and pieces as retold by others, but the firsthand accounts from P.J., C.C. and Alex—is a moment that I will never forget. My husband and I sat in Alex's room at Vanderbilt Stallworth with P.J., C.C., and Alex. We were chatting as we had every other visit when suddenly, as if they had told it a thousand times, the three of them started to recount their memories of the day of the accident. Where one would stop, another would pick up the story. We sat quietly, listening and holding back tears, as C.C. told of her fear when she received the phone call from the bystander who was first on the scene. As P.J. shared the unimaginable sights they saw as they arrived at the accident scene. As Alex told of the comfort he tried so desperately to give his brothers as they waited for help to arrive. It was such a profound moment to hear them begin to tell their story...

Melissa Wray, P.J.'s sister-in-law

—◦◦◦—

There is one simple way to start living again. Only one solution to this problem. Include God in your day. Even for five minutes. Give Him those minutes so that He can remind you HOW to live again, as He has reminded me. I would love to say that after the accident I gained a lasting knowledge of not taking my time for granted. But I am human, and no matter how hard our lessons in life are, sometimes God has to give us gentle reminders. He loves us enough to forgive us and welcome us back into His embrace.

June 2, 2016 (Blog Post)

Today, I made a Facebook post that I was no longer going to write my blog to avoid offending people. It was a quick decision made in the heat of the moment. I have never had to face persecution based on words that I write or thoughts that I have until now. I quickly discovered it isn't a great feeling. Although what I wrote was true, someone became offended by my post because it showed them in a negative light. So, I backed down and gave in to the fear of rejection.

Luckily, I have friends on Facebook who quickly jerked me to my senses. They were so right! To allow others to stop me from writing what I feel God wants me to share is to allow the devil to win. I have never been a quitter, and I refuse to become one now. I will not bow down to others or allow them to control what I do or say.

I do not regret posting what I did on Facebook, because in doing so I was able to see that my blog HAS been an inspiration to others. I truly didn't know how many took the time to read it, much less gained inspiration from what I have written. That was always the hope of course, and considering that God has lead me here to this point, I should have known better. He always has a plan and purpose. It was selfish of me to even consider quitting, and I won't do so again.

I am so thankful for all of you and your encouragement. It never hurts to have friends that are willing to put you in your place!

Until next time…

June 3, 2016 (Blog Post)

I sometimes wonder if bill collectors think that I am lying about not having the money to pay them. Like, seriously…I am totally making it up. I have a ton of money in the bank but I love that you call me five times a day as well as ALL the other people calling to collect money. I totally pay my cell phone bill just so that I can converse on the phone with bill collectors all day long. You're getting an attitude with me? Yeah, that isn't going to magically produce the money to pay you either. By the way, threatening me by saying it will reflect on my credit score doesn't scare me anymore. It can join all the others listed in alphabetical order.

Being business owners obviously has its benefits. We were lucky enough to be able to be with our boys after the accident, without fear of being fired from our jobs. There was also so many people who donated to the GoFundMe account. Had they not done so, we would have lost everything. We wouldn't have even been able to eat. Literally.

That money in large part was also used to do repairs to the house to make it wheelchair accessible for Jackson. So many promised to do things that they simply couldn't or didn't have the time to do. It ended up being a huge undertaking, especially financially. I seriously cannot express the amount of gratitude that our family has for everyone who gave when our family needed it the most. Without it, we wouldn't have been able to make it through.

The downside to being a business owner…you don't make money when you can't work. We didn't work for almost half a year. And sometimes when you own your own business, you still don't make money. It is the nature of being self-employed. I tried to take on a full-time job the first of the year but realized very quickly that I was needed with my family more. There are just too many doctor appointments with Jackson and Alex to allow me to work full-time.

I used to be the type of person to never discuss financial matters with anyone. Now, why wouldn't I share with those very people who gave and allowed us to stay in the hospital with our babies when so many other parents had to make the choice to leave their children to work? And seriously, if someone wanted to judge us considering all that we have been through as a family, I wouldn't want to be friends with them anyway.

I hate having to explain to bill collectors that we simply don't have the money to pay them. I hate calling my husband to tell him that they turned the water off. Or that a notice is on the front door and if we don't pay the electric within twenty-four hours, they are turning that off too. I used to have a great credit score. So being in this position now isn't fun. We don't chose to not pay bills. We just simply DON'T have it.

However, with all the financial difficulties our family has faced since the accident, I am also more thankful than I have ever been in my life. We may not be able to pay all our bills, and we may lose everything yet. But our kids are still here and alive, and at the end of the day, that really and truly is all that matters. Amazing how almost losing the most precious gift God can give you puts things into perspective. And no matter how many collection calls I get, if the call isn't to tell me that my boys have been in an accident, I will take them too.

So, if you are reading this and are one of those who simply can't make ends meet, cut yourself some slack. Take a moment to remember what you do have to be thankful for. No matter how broke we have been, our children have never been hungry. God will provide somehow, someway. He always does. Just hand it over to Him.

June 19, 2016 (Blog Post)
Yesterday I experienced one of the most embarrassing moments of my life, in front of customers nonetheless. I don't usually cry, but yesterday the tears just wouldn't stop.

I have been praying ceaselessly for God to give me direction on what I should do with my store, Vintage. It takes time to establish a business in a new location and because of the accident we simply don't have the capital we need to sustain it. My husband's auto repair business just isn't making the funds to provide for itself and our family so there has been added pressure for Vintage to provide an income, which it has not been able to do.

This weekend was a make it or break it opportunity. We would either make enough money to get ahead or we wouldn't. I poured everything I had in to it. As it is only myself and my assistant, we worked tirelessly in the heat preparing for the RC Moon Pie Festival in hopes that we would have a profitable weekend. My body aches like it hasn't in years.

In the meantime, I have also been seeking a job. There are many reasons why this wasn't my favorite choice, but the most important reason is I will be unable to be with my family. For me to make any type of money, I will have to take a job in Nashville or somewhere equivalent. This means leaving home at 6 o'clock in the morning and returning at six or seven o'clock in the evening. I will not be able to take our boys to the doctor, or pick Jackson up from school when he isn't feeling well, which happens a lot. I will also not be able to continue writing my book. As fate would have it, I was offered a job on Friday in Nashville, while preparing for this make it or break it weekend.

Sometimes God answers us, and it isn't always what we want to hear. That embarrassing moment was the final nail in the coffin so to speak. My heart simply cannot continue to take that type of embarrassment or disappointment. I can't continue to strive to do what I love while not being able to provide for my family. Right now, my children need me.

Someone made a comment on my post about how blessed I am. I should remember that I have my children and a husband who loves me. Yes, I am beyond blessed to have my children and thank God for them every single day. But there has been so much more heartache in my life that most couldn't begin to imagine. I know that God is using me to help others, but I pray that people also remember that in order for me to have this voice and this level of faith, it has taken insurmountable pain and a lifetime of experiences to earn it. Not just from the accident, but even as a little child.

I am not perfect. I wish I could be positive and uplifting while I give up the one dream I have ever had the courage to go after. Right now, all I can feel is heartache and sadness. I know that God has a purpose and a plan for my boys. For them I would do or give up anything. And I am, but it doesn't mean that my heart enjoys making sacrifices. I will do my best to process this as best I can and overcome as I always have, and I know that God will help me through. I just ask that if you can, say a prayer for me in the meantime.

June 27, 2016 "Let God Bless You"

Today, Pastor Randy of Life Restoration Church sent me a Facebook message inviting me to church service this morning. I immediately replied that I couldn't come because I was moving my store. His response? "If you come this morning, I will send a team of young men to help you move today. And you can come to church, and get filled up by the Holy Spirit, get a word from the Lord, and get some help at your store today." I immediately replied, Deal! Not because I expected anyone to help, but I figured that if he was that willing to get me to church, then God obviously had a word for me that I needed to hear.

When our lives are falling apart, church should be the first place we run. Me? I am hard-headed to the core. I try micro-managing everything by myself. I become a doer. I think that if I work hard enough I can fix it myself. Of course, I never do, and everything continues to fall down around me until I finally have to hand it over to God, which I should have done from the beginning.

Growing up, I had to be tough. I learned to be independent and strong. It has gotten me through a lot of trials, but it has also been one of my biggest flaws. I don't know how to ask for help. I just do it myself. Now ask me if I do it quietly or without anger? Nope, my feelings get hurt because people I love don't want to help me. My anger just pushes me forward until yes, the job is done, but I am one bitter person. Did I mention I can hold a grudge? Like, forever? It is another one of those flaws I am working on.

After church, Pastor Randy messaged me and said, "Hey! I got about ten men ready here!! Where are you?" I explained that he really didn't have to help, I came because I knew God had a word for me. He said, "You HAVE to let God bless you!!" Isn't it amazing how God wants to bless us, but we are the ones in His way stopping Him? He was right, and I knew it. God can't bless me when I won't let Him.

Why is it so hard to hand things over to Him? I wish I could tell all you that almost losing my boys brought me to a place of total trust and faith. I am and always will be a work in progress. Did I mention that the message today was about faith? One of the things Pastor Randy said was exactly what I needed to hear, "The harder the thing is that you have to go through, the more magnificent your testimony." God knew I needed the reminder. I needed to hear the words. Immediately after the accident, God told me that He had a plan and a purpose for this happening. I held on to His Word and it helped get me through one of the most difficult experiences of my life. I knew then that what our boys were going through was for His testimony.

Someone reminded me this week that God is using me for His purpose. My story and my voice has helped others, and continues to do so. It seems like my dream of Vintage is ending, but God has bigger plans in the works. And that when you use your voice to give God the praise, the devil comes in to try to steal it. I refuse to shut up. I have said it from the beginning, and I still say it. God has done too much for my family to not get the praise He deserves.

Not just ten young guys come to help, it was more like twenty. They had trucks and they were ready to work! I had spent four days packing and moving what I could in the back of my Tahoe, and had barely made a dent. What would have taken myself and Heather (who has been so good to me and agreed to stay to help me until the very end) two weeks to do took them a few hours. They literally moved my entire store with me. I cannot begin to express my gratitude.

While I was watching them fellowship with one another and moving furniture, God reminded me that what I was witnessing was church. Church is belonging to a family that loves one another. Belonging to a family of believers that loves people that they don't even know. These people didn't have to spend their Sunday afternoon in the sweltering heat to help someone they had barely met move. Yet they did, full of love and with no questions asked. They loved on me and encouraged me the entire time. And God did I need it! At the end of the day, they prayed with my husband and me. This group of young men are what church is all about. If you don't have a church family, I highly recommend Life Restoration Church.

As I showed them the car that the boys were in the accident in so that they could see why we were having to close my store and move furniture, God reminded me of the things I was grateful for. My heart aches because I had to give up my dream, but I must have faith and trust in God that this isn't the end. Our journey isn't over. We still have a long way to go. We have had to make many sacrifices as a family, and I am sure there will be more to make in the future.

Do I wish that our lives were back to "normal?" Absolutely! Would I love to be without all the stress I have endured for the last ten months? You bet I would! But I also would have missed out on all the good things that has come from the accident: hearing Jackson talk about his trip to Heaven, watching God work miracles time after time. Learning to let go and allowing Him to bless me! Hearing from people whose lives have forever been changed because of our family's story, and having a group of young men show up to not only help me move, but to love on me when I needed it the most and to remind me that I should have handed it over to God from the very beginning.

July 1, 2016 (Blog Post)

For the first time in fifteen years I do not have a cellular device, Internet, or cable TV. At first, the boys were horrified. Poor Jackson cried because he couldn't play his games online. Every day they asked if it was getting turned back on. Out of desperations, they started pulling board games out of the closet. They started to play using their imagination, instead of constantly playing video games. Jackson even admitted that it wasn't so bad not having Internet and they were having "fun" playing. They were forced to get creative, and that isn't such a bad thing. They even admitted that they enjoyed it.

It has been an experience for me as well. We often wonder what we would do without technology, and I have had the opportunity to learn firsthand. The only time I have access to the Internet is through my husband's mobile hotspot. It is nice not having to check my phone every ten minutes of the day. I am OCD and unread notifications drive me insane. Now, I only see them when I can connect. It is frustrating however, when I need to be connected to reach a customer or reply to an e-mail. I cannot even print documents because literally everything must have Wi-Fi to work.

When my two oldest sons were growing up I would never speak of finances with my them. I believed: speak as though you have instead of what you don't have. Your words are powerful so don't proclaim negative. My answer was simply no or not right now. As they became older, I realized I wasn't really teaching them truth. It is okay to teach children that not all of their wants are in the budget. Children need to understand that some things are luxuries, like Internet and cable, even though we believe we must have them. They too will have to make sacrifices, learn to budget their money and make smart decisions someday. I pray that they are all so successful that they don't have to go without anything, but the reality is at some point they will have to choose between paying the mortgage or electricity bill over buying the newest iPhone. I hope as parents we are teaching them the foundation of that concept.

Through it all I have learned that I can indeed survive without technology, but it is a luxury I enjoy and will be happy to have again we can afford to do so.

Before the accident, I would have never shared something like this. Now, I feel the need to be brutally honest. The reality is we are still struggling from the aftermath of the accident and the impact it has had on our lives and our finances. But even if that wasn't the case, most people struggle to make ends meet. Parents must decide how to use those times to teach positive example instead of feeling shame about their circumstances. I hope that by sharing our story others know they are not alone out there, and just maybe it will make their day a little better.

July 14, 2016 (Blog Post)

When I was a little girl, a woman came by our apartment in the projects of downtown Nashville to invite me to church. She told me about all the fun things the youth did at church and promised to come get me on the bus every Sunday. And she did. Her name was Lana Banana (although I am sure that wasn't her real name). I loved going to church where I learned about Jesus and His love for me. It was something to look forward to every week, and she gave me candy every time I walked onto that bus.

A couple of years later, the owner at a furniture store that we broke down in front of told me about Jesus and I told him I went to church on Sunday's. He gave me a stuffed doll that I cherished and invited me to visit his church. I told him I would, but I was maybe eight years old at the time and didn't have a way to get there. It was the first promise I ever remember breaking. It hurt to break that promise and I learned going forward to never again promise something that I couldn't do. He told me I was special and was going to do great things in life. No one had ever told me this, and I believed him.

A few years later, we moved from Nashville to Shelbyville. My great uncle Chuck came to visit and invited me to church with him. He picked me up every single Sunday. He paid for me to go to church camp when I was thirteen years old, where I accepted Jesus Christ into my heart.

Why did I share this? Because it was those people who helped lead me to salvation. Not one person. Not one experience. But several. Lana Banana, the driver of that church bus who came to the roughest projects in Nashville didn't know that I was ultimately saved. The owner of that furniture store couldn't have realized how special that doll was to me or the words of life he spoke into me. My uncle Chuck couldn't realize that by sowing the money to send me to church camp would ultimately lead me to the cross and salvation.

I'm not sure if I have ever been instrumental in someone's journey to become saved. I hope that I have been. And I hope that all who read this are reminded that every time you share Jesus with someone, speak words of life and encouragement into someone, or sow financially into ministry, you too may have been one of the people God used to help someone eventually reach salvation, without even knowing it.

July 26, 2016 (Blog Post)

When anniversaries are coming up, we tend to think about that moment in our lives that define that anniversary. If it's a wedding anniversary, we think about the day of our wedding and the memories made. On birthdays of our children, we remember our labor and delivery. The first moment we held our child and heard their cry. When anniversaries of the death of a loved one draws near, we think about the day we lost someone that we dearly loved. Anniversaries are place markers in our lives that have significant meaning. Sometimes, these dates changed the course of our lives forever.

With the anniversary of the accident fast approaching, I have spent a lot of time in thought. I have contemplated every decision that lead up to that horrific day. A day that will forever be considered the worst day in my life. My life was forever changed. Our children's lives were forever changed. It was literally my worst nightmare, except one that I couldn't wake up from. I had to live it. I had to face it. I was mom, and failing wasn't an option. I had five children who needed me. I remember thinking, "I have to do this. I have to be strong for them." And on the tail of that thought, "God, please give me the strength to do this."

The last week has been extremely hard for me. The memories sometimes take me back to that phone call. Being on the side of that road, hearing my children scream. The helplessness that I felt. Seeing them in pain, and not being able to take it away. Those first days in the hospital when we didn't know if Alex or Jackson would live. The moment when the doctor told us that Jackson would never walk again.

But there are also good memories. The strength of family. The outpouring of love from strangers who supported us every step of the way. The miracles, time after time, that God bestowed on our babies. The opportunity for us to grow as individuals and lessons learned, like humility and faith.

This anniversary will always define the day our lives changed. It will be, according to doctors, the last day that Jackson will ever walk again. There will always be sadness and "what ifs." Yet, God reminded me that in this too I have a choice. I can choose to dwell on the heartache. I can choose to remember as a mother the overwhelming fear that I had. Or I can choose to remember the good. I can remember the love and support we were shown. The moments when God showed up and showed out. Our front row seats as He showed us what faith and prayer can do. I can be thankful that all our boys are here. And I can cherish every single moment I have been allowed to share with them. Each smile. Each laugh. The chance to be there for every single accomplishment they have achieved on their journey, because these boys of mine are strong and they are fighters.

So, as the anniversary draws near, I will remember the good and to be thankful for what God has done.

CHAPTER 16

—※—

I see that the Lord is always with me. I will
not be shaken, for he is right beside me. No
wonder my heart is glad, and my tongue
shouts his praises! My body rests in hope.

ACTS 2:25–26 NLT

July 30, 2016 (Blog Post)

THERE WAS AN old crate from a factory in Nashville that I absolutely loved. I had huge plans of making it into a flower planter. Jackson, however, decided he needed to tear it apart with tools. He is going through a phase of wanting to build things and using his imagination to think of alternate uses for items. I want to encourage this kind of learning in normal circumstances. My vintage crate had an intended use, and it definitely wasn't meant to be broken into pieces.

Jackson hardly ever gets in trouble, but this morning I had to lecture him about respecting other people's personal property. I explained to him that this was something that I loved and it can never be replaced.

It has always been hard to discipline Jackson. When he was little he would look at me with his big blue eyes and say, "I sorry." It is even more difficult now. And yet, it has to be done. Regardless of his circumstances, he still must learn what acceptable behavior is.

Had the culprit been one of our other boys, the punishment would have been more severe than a lecture. Jacob would have been expected to know better. Joshua as well, but he is still at the age where he makes mistakes and does things without thinking of the consequences. With Jackson, a lecture was enough. With tears in his eyes, he apologized and sincerely meant it.

One of these days, a lecture won't be enough. He will grow older, come into puberty and all the teenage drama that entails. Although disciplining him will still be difficult, I pray that I step up to the challenge. At the end of the day, regardless if he is in a wheelchair or not, I am responsible for teaching him. It is my job to make sure that his knows right from wrong, how to treat others, and always strives to be the best that he can be.

As we always say, Jackson is the same now as he was before the car accident, he just gets around on wheels instead of two legs. That means treating him the same and having the same expectations as we do for all our other boys.

August 29, 2016 (Blog Post)

Yesterday, we were finally able to meet the emergency response teams that helped save our boys lives on August 16, 2015. It was such a terrific experience for all of us. They took the time to clarify assumptions that we had such as we thought Jackson and Alex were the last to be airlifted to Vanderbilt when indeed they were the first. Alex did insist that they get his brothers out of the vehicle first. They remarked on how much the brothers cared for one another. They were each concerned about their brothers as they were extracted from the vehicle. We knew it was a miracle that Jacob is capable of walking today, but after hearing about the complexity of his extraction and the severity of his injuries, it is even more apparent now. They showed the boys the tools that were used to help get them out of the vehicle. Allowed them to see inside of the fire truck and ambulances, and even ride in the fire truck. The heroes from Rutherford County Fire Dept., EMS, and SORT Team went above and beyond the call of duty on that fateful day. They continued to care about our boy's well-being, even after their job was done. I am forever grateful to each and every one of them.

September 4, 2016 (Blog Post)

I was finally baptized today. I am not sure how I always managed to miss my church baptisms. Maybe I was in the bathroom when it was announced, or I didn't take the time to read the handout with monthly church activities posted. Inevitably, I somehow always missed it. Until today.

A few weeks ago, God put it on my heart to ask my pastor to baptize me. But isn't that what baptism is? A covenant that we should seek instead of it being at a convenient time in our lives? It is up to us to pursue Him. Yes, I once again missed the announcement somehow. But it wasn't a coincidence that I was tagged in a Facebook post letting everyone know at our church that this Sunday would be a baptism service. God knew I was ready to seek Him and He opened the door to make it happen.

As I was waiting for the baptisms begin, I felt very alone. My church family loved on me, of course. But I wanted my husband and my children there with me. This was one of the biggest moments of my life. Who would take a picture of this moment?!? Who would I talk to about what I was feeling after it was over? Then God whispered, "Me." He reminded me that this was about my relationship and covenant with Him and Him alone. No matter what I go through in life, He is always there and I am never truly alone. All I can do is continue to love my family and be there for the important moments in their lives. Love them through actions. Yes, my heart was sad that they chose not to be there, but thankfully I have a Father who is always there.

November 2, 2016 (Blog Post)

After spending the day at Vanderbilt with Jackson to start his bone infusions, I was reminded that gender, race, financial status, or even what church you attend means nothing at all.

My heart broke for all of the children there receiving chemo or infusions. Children of different ethnic backgrounds. Children of parents who had little in the way of money, and children from parents who had more than enough. I saw a girl who could hardly move and had no hair left. A child no older than six throwing up but refusing help and insisting to her concerned parents that she was okay. I watched a mother rolling her child around in a wheelchair for hours to distract her. I saw babies and I saw teenage boys just barely old enough to drive. I watched volunteers hand out toys, drinks, and snacks. Doing whatever they could to help cheer and encourage these little patients. It didn't matter if the child was a girl or a boy. If their parents were rich or poor. If their skin was black or white.

In this they were all one. All fighting to stay alive. They were equals.

If only everyone who thought their race or the amount of money they had in the bank made them better than others could visit the 6th floor at Vanderbilt Children's Hospital, it would change the world.

December 31, 2016 (Blog Post)

If you're human and have a pulse, chances are you have been thinking back on what you did this year and most assuredly what you didn't do. Millions of dollars are spent by big corporations to remind you that you should have a resolution and that this is THE year for you to keep it! Everyone on social media is talking about their goals and what they've already accomplished or plan to accomplish in the new year. Better yet, there are "those" people that make sure to announce they don't do New Year's resolutions. And seriously, how many memes about New Year's could there possibly be? You know, the ones designed to make you contemplate your life's purpose and just for a second you think you really can aspire to achieve it? Until real-life sets in of course.

With all of that, how could I not be thinking about my last year and everything I learned and did? I should warn you that this is not one of those posts meant to inspire you into greatness just by reading it. The things I learned this year were real-life lessons. Some good, some bad. The truth is, that is real life. It isn't always all rainbows and sunshine. Life is great, but with it comes heartbreak and loss.

The hardest thing I learned this year? Giving up on your dream, even if temporarily, sucks. Like…a lot. I remember reading an article about Joanne Gaines and how she decided to close her very first storefront to be a stay-at-home mom. Of course, now she is a super star running a multimillion dollar business. I wonder if she easily transitioned to both roles with as much grace and ease as it sounded in that article. If she had those moments when she thought she would go crazy if she couldn't be around other adults for one more single day. I knew that being at home with the boys was where God wanted me to be. I simply couldn't be at my store without feeling guilty about not being with my boys, nor could I be with them without thinking about all I needed to do at the store. By nature, I am an overachiever who needs stay busy. I must have goals and something to achieve. It was difficult to switch gears so completely and abruptly. Being a stay-at-home mom is hard. You don't earn a paycheck and in most cases, you aren't even thanked for all that you do. But my point is this: just because we are where God needs us to be doesn't mean it's going to be easy. Sometimes, it is harder. But it is in those places that we are able to grow and to learn the most.

A few other things I learned this year?

It is okay to have days when it is simply too much work to put make-up on and fix your hair. This is totally acceptable. However, it isn't acceptable to *not* brush your teeth or brush your hair. It is not okay to wear pajamas in public. For God's sake, please don't wear pajamas in public…

It is okay to be late or accidently miss an appointment. Believe it or not, the world does not shift course on its axis. It actually happened to me and I assure you, the world kept on turning.

It's okay not to have a clean house every single day. Really, how many people ever actually come to your house to even know if it's clean or not??? And if you're OCD and you actually do want your house clean every single day like me, it's okay to own that too. As I told my husband, being OCD is my coping mechanism so he is just going to have to deal with it. A clean house never killed anyone!

I am never going to be the person I want to be. Sounds melodramatic, doesn't it? But the truth is, we should always strive to be better than we are right now. Why was this such an important revelation to me? I am not perfect. There, I said it. And guess what? Neither are you. Isn't that so freeing? It is okay to be who you are, right this very minute.

Some friends, even the ones we think will always be there, won't. They will hurt you deeply and you simply have to learn to let go.

It's entirely appropriate to scream at people while sometimes showing them your bird finger when driving because they are an idiot and shouldn't have a license. Well, perhaps not but as I just pointed out, I'm not perfect.

I don't have to fit my body into midrise jeans when high-rise jeans are so much more comfortable. That's all.

It is okay to sometimes want to stab your significant other in the eye with a fork. Because there is no way I am the only one who has thought this. Right?!?! My point is, marriage is sometimes hard. Life isn't all rainbows and sunshine, as mentioned above. Life is real and let's face it, sometimes crappy. It is why we vow until death do us part. There are days when we don't feel "the love." And that's okay too.

I hope that if you too have spent time thinking about your life this year and where you want to be, you have been able to accept that who you are is exactly who you were meant to be.

March 23, 2017 (Blog Post)
Going to Vanderbilt Children's Hospital still feels in part like coming home. You would think that being there would bring all of the negative memories rushing back like running down the hallway to where each child was located to find out how badly each was hurt. Receiving the news that Jackson would never walk again. Holding Alex's hand as he screamed from the pain of Acute Compartment Syndrome. The sleepless nights, and day after day of countless surgeries. I experienced the most frightening moments of my life inside of those doors.

And yet, what I remember above all else when I am back at Vanderbilt is the hope I felt as God answered prayer after prayer. Learning that our family was loved by many…more than I could ever have even possibly imagined. The kindness and generosity of strangers. The power of love and the strength of family. The importance of prayers, even those that seem hopeless. The lessons I learned about life. The testing and growing of my faith. The comfort of knowing that we were in the care of more than capable hands.

So, while Jackson and I were at his 6-month check-up with his spinal surgeon this week, I leaned on that comfort as the doctor explained that Jackson would have to have another spinal fusion in a year and a half, possibly sooner. It wasn't what we wanted to hear. I sometimes forget that our journey isn't over. There will be more surgeries, more medical scares. Alex and Jackson's lives will never be what they were before the wreck. But we keep pressing forward, having faith that God will get us through whatever lies ahead. As I told Jackson yesterday as we all huddled in the closet during pretty severe storms, Jesus didn't save you and take you to Heaven for nothing. You have a purpose here on earth and no storm is going to change that.

—Ⓦ—

CHAPTER 17

*I am leaving you with a gift—peace of mind and
heart. And the peace I give is a gift the world
cannot give. So don't be troubled or afraid.*

JOHN 14:27 NLT

OUR JOURNEY HAS been long, and in many ways, we have a long way
yet to go. There are always more surgeries to think about. Emotional
hurdles to cross. One moment in time changed our lives forever. Yet
despite all the hardship we have been through, there have also been
great moments. Life lessons learned. A family that was once broken,
even before the accident, is finally together as a whole again. Yes, I wish
that bad things never happened to anyone. But the truth is, they do and
they will. At the end of the day, it's what we choose to learn from those
difficult times that define who we are. We don't get to choose how
every moment of our life will play out. We will experience pain and
heartbreak. We will lose those we love. It is the nature of life. But we
do get to choose whether we believe in God. We can choose to lean on
Him when life gets hard. We can choose to find the good in every situation, because no matter how difficult life can be, there is always good.

On a hot day on August 16, 2015, God told me he had a plan and
a purpose for our lives. He told me, "I've got this." And He did,

in every way imaginable. During every trial our family faced, He was there. During every sleepless night, He was by my side. When all seemed hopeless, He offered us hope and reassurance. When it seemed impossible, He made the possible happen. I am not saying that those months were without pain, fear, and despair. I'm not trying to make you believe that I was a rock-star Christian with the faith to move mountains. What I want you to know is that I was a normal, everyday mom who had the same fears and doubts as any other person. I wasn't strong, but He was. There were days He literally had to hold me up and sometimes push me forward, because I didn't think I could take one more step.

I know that Alex will someday preach the Word. I believe that through all the physical and emotional trauma, God was building up a mighty warrior. He has been preparing Alex all along. Alex has such a love for others, and I know that love will be used to help bring others to Christ someday. I simply can't wait to sit on the front pew to hear him preach!

Jackson will tell you that Jesus saved him, and He did. For Jackson, it is not really that big a deal. He died, went to Heaven, and came back again. Of course, I know there is more to it than that. Jackson has a purpose in this life, and I believe he too will someday share Jesus with the world. Jackson's eyes light up when he talks about the love he felt in Heaven. The beautiful things he saw. There is so much more about his trip to Heaven that he hasn't shared with us yet. Someday, he will share his story with everyone who is willing to listen. I don't know if Jackson will walk again. Do I want him to be able to stand on his own two feet? Sure I do. But I also know that Jackson will fulfill God's plan for his life whether standing or sitting on two wheels. Jackson's life will be full and happy, because God said it was so, and God never breaks his promises.

The Beginning...

WHEN GOD FIRST asked me to write this book, my first response was, "You've got to be kidding, right?" Nope. He was most definitely not. It took a lot of nudging on His part for me to finally listen, and even more so to convince me to share such personal information about my life and our family. I knew in my heart that our story needed to be shared so I decided to just take a leap of faith. Amazing how God is always there to catch us, isn't it? I've believed since the beginning of our journey that it was never just about "us". I hope that by reading our family's story, your life has been touched in some tangible way.

I would love for you to continue following our family's journey at theroadwaytoheaven.com and facebook.com/theroadwaytoheaven. Hope to see you there!

Love & blessings,

C.C. Hasty Andrews